The Garden

Bella Akhmadulina

NEW AND SELECTED POETRY AND PROSE

Edited, Translated, and
Introduced by F. D. Reeve

Marion Boyars
London • New York

Copyright © 1973, 1974, 1977, 1983, 1987, 1988, 1990
by Bella Akhmadulina
Translation copyright © 1990 by F. D. Reeve
All rights reserved.
First published in Great Britain in 1991 by
Marion Boyars Publishers Ltd,
24 Lacy Road, London SW15 1NL.
Distributed in Australia by
Wild & Woolley, Glebe, N.S.W.

British Library Cataloguing in Publication Data available.
ISBN 0-7145-2924-9 original paperback edition

Designed by Claire Naylon Vaccaro

Printed in the United States of America

10 9 8 7 6 5 4 3 2 1

353616

O magic theater of a poem . . .

СОДЕРЖАНИЕ

Поэзия

Сад	2
Кофейный чертик	6
Заклинание	10
Клянусь	12
Варфоломеевская ночь	16
«Есть тайна у меня от чудного цветенья»	20
Снимок	24
Дачный роман	28
«Стихотворения чудный театр»	38
Сказка о дожде	40
Озноб	64
Приметы мастерской	74
«Не уделяй мне много времени»	78
«Прохожий, мальчик, что ты?»	80
Возвращение в Тарусу	82
«Кто знает — вечность или миг»	84
Ладыжино	86
Два гепарда	90
Шум тишины	92
Звук указующий	96
Елка в больничном коридоре	98
Сад/всадник	102
«Чудовищный и призрачный курорт»	106
Другое	112
Строка	114
День-Рафаэль	116

CONTENTS

Introduction   xi

Poetry

The Garden   3
The Coffee Imp   7
An Incantation   11
I Swear   13
Saint Bartholomew's Day   17
[The Secret]   21
The Photograph   25
A Summer-House Love Story   29
[Poetry Magic]   39
A Fairy Tale About Rain   41
Chills   65
Features of an Artist's Studio   75
[Don't Spend a Lot of Time on Me]   79
[Hey, Kid!]   81
Return to Tarusa   83
[Who Knows]   85
Ladyzhino   87
Two Cheetahs   91
The Noise of Silence   93
Sound Pointing the Way   97
The Hospital Christmas Tree   99
The Garden / The Guardsman   103
[Olgino]   107
Something Else   113
The Line   115
Raphael's Day   117

«В том времени, где и злодей»   118

Смерть совы   122

«Всех обожаний бедствие огромно»   128

«Ночь: белый сонм колонн надводных»   130

«Я думала, что ты мой враг»   132

«Всё шхеры, фиорды, ущельных существ»   134

«Я завидую ей — молодой»   140

Театр   144

[In Memory of O. Mandelshtam]   119
An Owl's Death   123
[The Fog]   129
[The Echo]   131
[Parting]   133
[Sortavala]   135
[Anna Akhmatova]   141
The Theater   145

Prose

A Word That Amounts to a Deed   149
Babushka   151
An Eternal Presence   165

... This symbol is used to indicate a space between stanzas of a poem wherever such spaces are lost in pagination.

INTRODUCTION

Bella Akhmadulina stands out among contemporary Russian poets for her broad range, firm technique, and spiritual vision. Russian critics tend to label their poets "formalist" or "acmeist" or "social realist," and we tend to pigeonhole them according to reputation: the greater the publicity, the more we esteem the author even without understanding the original text. The more Russian poets visit America, however, the more we discover Russia's poetic achievements and the ways they express what Diaghilev called "the unconscious nationalism of the blood."

Noticed after the appearance of her teenage poems in 1955 and celebrated for the originality and independence of her voice with publication of her first book *Struna (The String,* 1962), in the post-Khrushchev era Akhmadulina suffered expulsion from the Soviet Writers' Union and then reinstatement as a translator, but her poetry continued to appear in major Soviet journals from Moscow's *October, Youth,* and *Literary Gazette* to the provincial *Literary Georgia* and *Star of the East.* The emotional intensity, the verbal wit, and the narrative strength of her work earned her national respect. When spiritual life is suppressed, she told *The Harvard Advocate* in May 1988, "people turn to the poet as confessor and priest." When a nation has Russia's difficulties, she added, "people seek something lofty, something spiritual. And that's why people are always striving for what's beautiful, lofty, musical."

The present volume, opening with the title poem of her 1987 collection *Sad (The Garden)* and including many poems not previously published in English, draws on the whole body of her work, from that first collection through *Oznob (Chills,* 1968), *Metel' (The Snowstorm,* 1977), *Sny o Gruzii (Dreams of Georgia,* 1977), *Taina (The Secret,* 1983), and *The Garden* to *Izbrannoe (Selected Poems,* 1988). Critics have called her poetry classical, pointing out its use of rhyme, meter, and standard prosodic patterns. In the course of thirty years, however, her poetry has changed, expanding its themes and ranging its diction from archaic to slang. At the same time, the idea of classicism has evolved. The Romantics rebelled against neoclassicism; then the Romantic landscape of pond and willows, marble fauns, and lazy clouds became classical itself, both a standard of excellence and a cause for rebellion by the Symbolists, the Acmeists, the Futurists, all the poets of modernism. In turn, the poetry of Blok, Pasternak, Mandelshtam, and Akhmatova, with its visions of a lost but structured world, became the classical standard against which the postwar poets had to craft their attitudes and create their identities. For Akhmadulina, the world of a poem is a sumptuous estate on which, as in Chekhov's *The Cherry Orchard*, someone is always cutting down the trees.

Because Pushkin more than anyone else established classical Russian diction—the ordinary language of literature—only one hundred and fifty years ago and because a poet's competence can be judged by prosodic skill, every Russian poet offers a self-evaluation through his/her response to Pushkin. The abler the poet, the greater the respect and the bolder the modernization. Born one hundred years after Pushkin's death, Akhmadulina has cloaked her spirit with his, has made him *her* secret Pushkin. "An Eternal Presence" clearly states her attitude and reminds us of two points: The genuine poet's public life of duty, debt, scandal, guilt, and notoriety is a travesty of the workings of the spirit, and for a Russian poet literary tradition is more significant than political convention or rights to liberty and property.

Freedom means writing as well as one can within the tradition. To deny tradition is to deny one's own spirit and one's very language. Akhmadulina consciously used Pushkin's title "My Genealogy" for one of her poems and imagined herself by candlelight back in Pushkin's time. In her nature poetry she repeatedly and evocatively echoes Pushkin only to distance her modern self from him: autumn was Pushkin's favorite season; in a poem about October Akhmadulina says that then "there's more Pushkin around, or, rather, only he remains both in nature and in one's head."

Her slang phrases bounce off her archaisms and her jeweled syntax. All important twentieth-century Russian poets have used archaisms, Church Slavonic forms, and elevated lexicons, but, as Sofiya Lyubenskaya commented, "Akhmadulina's handling of these linguistic layerings is exceptionally sophisticated."

A memoir of her grandmother, "Babushka," gives the kind of biographical information she would have us know. It does not matter, she seems to say, that she was married to Yevgeny Yevtushenko—she told one interviewer, "I've already forgotten I was married to him"—and Yury Nagibin, or that she is married to Boris Messerer. What matters is the magic the spirit makes, as in "Features of an Artist's Studio," dedicated to Messerer. What matters is the transformation of the past, as in "Rafael's Day," in which she transforms her Italian background on her mother's side into a poetic concept, the idea of Italy leads to Rafael, Rafael to his mural *Days and Hours* in the Vatican, and the scene to "a dead oak in the open valley," an image taken from a popular nineteenth-century Russian song. Tied into a cycle of winter poems, "Rafael's Day" is, like all her later poems, a web of recollection and invention.

What matters is what the spirits of time and place make as she associates her literary self with Marina Tsvetaeva in all the Tarusa references and with Anna Akhmatova in wartime evacuation and later, in nostalgic northern elegies. She cites Aleksandr Blok, honors Osip Mandelshtam, admires Bulat Okudzhava, looks on nature—which Akhmatova called Boris Pasternak's "secret interlocutor"—very much with Pasternak's attitude of impartiality toward events and reverence for mystery.

She lives in Moscow, gives readings throughout the Soviet Union, and recently has paid annual visits to the United States. Like many Russians in public performances, she recites her poems from memory with a grave, seemingly disinterested intensity, as if she were trying to get out of their way. The poems say little about her. The "I" in them is a lyric persona kept at arm's length to project her emotional discoveries. In "The Secret" and "The Garden," for example, the poet acts out roles of lexicographer, historian, and naturalist, but her chief role is remaker of consciousness, or keeper of the language. At first whimsically, later obstinately, she insists that real time is time remembered and that the imagination houses reality.

Throughout her poems there are not only obsolete spellings and religious terms but especially a sense of underlying, transcendent faith. The paraphernalia of nature—rivers, moonlit gardens, flowering cherries, even Goethe's Erlkönig borrowed from Tsvetaeva's version of the ballad using Zhukovsky's original translation—flesh out the nature poems, which are about exultation. Fields and forests, like human faces, are maskers in a play of trivial dialogue but of great spiritual import:

> We're con artists both. In the dead of the night,
> in time beyond time, the garden / the guardsman sails on.
> May the infant doomed to the Tsar of the Woods
> neither ever know fear nor ever be saved.

Images of suffering, as in "The Hospital Christmas Tree," "Saint Bartholomew's Day," and "Anna Akhmatova," and of surreal experience, as in "The Noise of Silence" and "Ladyzhino," express a radical awareness of social injustice transformed into spiritual resignation. "Their" suffering becomes hers in real life, too: for example, when asked if she was trying to save Sakharov by defending him to Western reporters, she replied, "No, I was trying to save my own conscience."

A poem such as "Two Cheetahs" takes off from a first line that replicates one of Tsvetaeva's to become sharp social commentary. Fiercely loyal to her heritage and proud of its accomplishments, Akhmadulina has spoken out against hypocrisy, deceit, corruption, and oppression without joining any movement or advocating any policy. Her deepest concern has been for artistic freedom so that the cultural tradition may continue its brilliance in the years ahead. For that to happen, the artist must be granted independence; independent, the artist must then assert his/her vision no matter how it contradicts the safe, comfortable patterns of established reality. The poem "The Theater" expresses her admiration for Vladimir Vysotsky, a powerful, for a long time underground, actor, later a popular but, alas, fatally alcoholic idol, whose performances helped make Moscow's Theater on the Taganka the center of artistic protest.

The Anacreontic tone of the poem on her husband's studio and of poems for such fellow poets as Andrei Voznesensky and Bulat Okudzhava—light verse praising conviviality—becomes playful in longer, narrative verse. Detached from herself, like Elwood P. Dowd from Harvey, she sets up a fond game with her partial double, putting it through fantastic hoops, screaming with excitement and giggling with pleasure as she goes:

> *Beat on me like a tambourine; don't spare me,*
> *chills—I'm wholly yours! Apart, I'm lost!*
> *I'm the ballerina of your music!*
> *I'm the frozen puppy of your frost!*

The humorous love-hate game with herself makes her different from her well-intentioned, middle-class neighbors, who cannot deal with visions or translate dreams. Most important, she did not elect difference; difference, like Rain, was thrust upon her. She responded compassionately, was later delighted to say different, nonconformist things. Behind the absurdities of social intercourse and her various guises is inarticulative self-consciousness and, privately, poods of guilt:

> *How much the liquor smells of roses! Or*
> *whatever; it alone is not at fault.*
> *In me the atom of the grape is split;*
> *in me there burns two different roses' war.*

Many of these themes, tones, mannerisms, and attitudes inform the poem "A Summer-House Love Story," a paragon of light verse—

> *Some moonlit night*
> *another half-mad lover might*
> *(if he's not too heavy for the ice*
> *just formed and can get through the dark)*
> *make his way up to my house.*

—but one in which the poet toys with her self-assigned role, intruding herself into the lives of her actors and then sublimating the game: suddenly we are dealing not with the tale of a love triangle at a dacha but with Akhmadulina, Pushkin, and Pushkin's lover Anna Kern, addressee of one of his exquisite lyrics. The ordinariness of the first imaginary triangle makes it seem real; the second, based partly on real life and on the reality of art, is so illusory that it seems plausible. Boxed in by its rules, packaged like a game, art is delightful—

> *Still, after centuries, just like that,*
> *we fall in love at the drop of a hat.*

—but unlike a game, it has real meaning:

> *sweetening verse with samples of*
> *the true and bitter taste of love.*

The spirit of love is the noblest, the simplest, the first and the last. With "Labor," "Liberty," and "Talent," it is one of the four cardinal points by which Akhmadulina steers, and it comes forth directly with magical defiance in such love poems as "Don't Spend a Lot of Time on Me," "Hey, Kid!," and "Parting." No matter how intricate or recondite her prosody or how challenging her dilemmas in longer poems, these small lyrics shine like stars in the dark sky of Russian literature from the past forty years.

The translations offered here are fairly close to the Russian in meaning, measure, and—much less so—rhyme. The original rhythms are mostly preserved, at times with metrical literalness. Because English is not inflected and Russian is, the rhyming is often suggestive, not imitative. Archaisms, neologisms, and some linguistic inventions carry one aspect of Akhmadulina's poetic characteristics. There are a few alterations or additions to the imagery of the originals; such textural corruptions occur in places where preserving rhyme or rhythm seemed more important—and, if done well, should be apparent only to people reading the original. Poems untitled in the Russian have been given bracketed titles in the English for convenience of reference.

Readers wishing to look more closely into Akhmadulina's poetry might turn to "The Wonder of Nature and Art" (in *New Studies in Russian Language and Literature,* Crone and Chvany, eds. [Columbus, Ohio, 1987]) and "Poetic Creation in Bella Axmadulina" (in *Slavic and East European Journal* 28, no. 1 [Spring 1984]), two articles by Sonia Ketchian of Harvard's Russian Research Center, who not only supplied some of the facts found in this Introduction but also kindly, spiritedly vetted the translations.

A celebrity in her own country, Akhmadulina once said, "I don't accept the love and adoration of my admirers as solely my own; I feel that it's for the great Russian poets who preceded me." As for Americans and American poets, she remarked, "I keep feeling there's somebody I haven't met yet." May this book bring the living Russian literary tradition closer to Americans—and Americans, to Akhmadulina.

Poetry

САД

Я вышла в сад, но глушь и роскошь
живут не здесь, а в слове «сад».
Оно красою роз возросших
питает слух, и нюх, и взгляд.

Просторней слово, чем окрестность:
в нем хорошо и вольно, в нем
сиротство саженцев окрепших
усыновляет чернозем.

Рассада неизвестных новшеств,
о слово «сад» — как садовод,
под блеск и лязг садовых ножниц
ты длишь и множишь свой приплод.

Вместилась в твой объем свободный
усадьба и судьба семьи,
которой нет, и той садовой
потерто-белый цвет скамьи.

Ты плодороднее, чем почва,
ты кормишь корни чуждых крон,
ты — дуб, дупло, Дубровский, почта
сердец и слов: любовь и кровь.

Твоя тенистая чащоба
всегда темна, но пред жарой
зачем потупился смущенно
влюбленный зонтик кружевной?

Не я ль, искатель ручки вялой,
колено гравием красню?

THE GARDEN

I went out to the garden—but in *garden,*
   the word, lies lush luxuriance.
As gorgeous as a full-blown rose, it
   enriches sound and scent and glance.

The word is wider than what surrounds me:
   inside it all is well and free;
its rich black soil makes sons and daughters
   of orphaned and transplanted seeds.

Seedlings of dark innovations,
   O *garden,* word, you are the gardener,
who to the clippers' gleam and clatter
   increase and spread the fruits you bear.

Set within your free-and-easy
   space are an old estate and the fate
of a family long gone, and the faded
   whiteness of their garden bench.

You are more fertile than the earth:
   you feed the roots of others' crowns.
From oak to oakwood, Oakboy, you are
   hearts' mail, and words'—the love, the blood.

Your shady grove is always darkened,
   but why did a lovelorn parasol
of lace look down in embarrassment
   in the face of hot weather coming on?

Perhaps I, who quest for a limp hand,
   redden my own knees on the stones?

Садовник нищий и развязный,
чего ищу, к чему клоню?

И если вышла, то куда я
все ж вышла? Май, а грязь прочна.
Я вышла в пустошь захуданья
и в ней прочла, что жизнь прошла.

Прошла! Куда она спешила?
Лишь губ пригубила немых
сухую муку, сообщила,
что все — навеки, я — на миг.

На миг, где ни себя, ни сада
я не успела разглядеть.
«Я вышла в сад», — я написала.
Я написала? Значит, есть

хоть что-нибудь? Да, есть, и дивно,
что выход в сад — не ход, не шаг.
Я никуда не выходила. Я просто
 написала так:
«Я вышла в сад»...

A casual and impoverished gardener,
    what do I seek? Where do I tend?

If I had gone out, where would I really
    have gone? It's May—and solid mud.
I went out to a ruined wasteland
    and in it read that life was dead.

Dead! Gone! Where had it hurried to?
    It merely tasted the dried-up agony
of speechless lips and then reported:
    all things forever; only a moment for me.

For a moment in which I could not manage
    to see either self or garden clearly.
"I went out to the garden" was what I wrote.
    I did? Well, then, there must be

something to it? There is—and amazing
    how going to the garden takes no move.
I did not go out at all. I simply wrote the
        way I usually do,
    "I went out to the garden . . ."

КОФЕЙНЫЙ ЧЕРТИК

Опять четвертый час. Да что это, ей-богу!
Ну, что четвертый час, о чем поговорим?
Во времени чужом люблю свою эпоху:
тебя, мой час, тебя, веселый кофеин.

Сообщник-гуща, вновь твой черный чертик ожил.
Ему пора играть, но мне-то — спать пора.
Но угодим ему. Ум на него помножим —
и то, что обретем, отпустим до утра.

Гадаешь ты другим, со мной — озорничаешь.
Попав вовнутрь судьбы, зачем извне гадать?
А если я спрошу, ты ясно означаешь
разлуку, не любовь, и ночи благодать.

Но то, что обрели, — вот парочка, однако.
Их общий бодрый пульс резвится при луне.
Стих вдумался в окно, в глушь снега и оврага.
И, видимо, забыл про чертика в уме.

Стих далеко летал, вернулся, но не вырос.
Пусть думает свое, ему всегда видней.
Ведь догадался он, как выкроить и выкрасть
Тарусу, ночь, меня из бесполезных дней.

Эй, чертик! Ты шалишь во мне, а не в таверне.
Дай помолчать стиху вблизи его луны.
Покуда он вершит свое самотворенье,
люблю на труд его смотреть со стороны.

Меня он никогда не утруждал нимало.
Он сочинит свое — я напишу пером.

THE COFFEE IMP

"Past three again! Honest to God, what are you doing?"
"So, it's after three—what'll we talk about?"
In a period that's alien I love the time that's mine:
you, special hour, and you, my cheery friend, caffeine.

Coffee grounds, accomplice, your black-faced imp has come
to life again: it's his time for playing; mine, for bed.
But let's satisfy him: we'll multiply our mind by him
and before dawn comes set free the answer in our head.

Others you tell fortunes; with me you just play tricks.
Once you know the outcome, why pretend to guess?
Yet if I ask directly, you flagrantly predict
a separation, no lovemaking, and night's amazing grace.

The answer we got—but here's a couple coming by.
Their bold and single heartbeat is quickened by the moon.
That verse composed itself from the snowscape out the window
and surely overlooked the imp that was on our mind.

It flew far off, returned but never really formed.
Let it think itself—it always knows what's best.
After all, it figured how to scissor out and snatch
Tarusa, night and me from countless, pointless days.

Hey, imp! It's me you're scampering in, not in some bar!
And let that verse keep quiet when it gets near his moon.
While he's working on his self-creation, I love to watch
the way he sweats but always keep myself aloof.

He never causes me the slightest bit of trouble.
He makes his own things up—I write in ballpoint black.

Забыла — дальше как? Как дальше, тетя Маня?
Ах, да, там дровосек приходит с топором.

Пока же стих глядит, что делает природа.
Коль тайну сохранит и не предаст словам —
пускай! Я обойдусь добычею восхода,
вы спали — я его сопроводила к вам.

Всегда казалось мне, что в достиженье рани
есть лепта и моя, есть тайный подвиг мой.
Я не ложилась спать, а на моей тетради
усталый чертик спит, поникнув головой.

Пойду, спущусь к Оке для первого поклона.
Любовь души моей, вдруг твой ослушник — здесь
и смеет говорить: нет воли, нет покоя,
а счастье — точно есть. Это оно и есть.

Wait, I've forgotten—what comes next? What, Aunty Manya?
Oh yes: *Here comes the woodsman with his heavy ax.*

Meanwhile, the verse turns watchful eye on nature's doings.
As long as it keeps mystery safe, not betraying it
to language, fine! I'll make do by catching the sunrise—
you lay sleeping—I was escorting it to you.

I've always thought that getting to an ungodly hour
is my own mite, my secret and mysterious feat.
Here, I haven't gone to bed, and on my notebook
a tired, droopy-headed imp is sound asleep.

I'll go down to the Oka to pay my first respects.
Your disobedient servant now, the love that lies
within me makes bold to speak: *There's no free will, no peace,
but there's good luck. That's precisely what this is.*

ЗАКЛИНАНИЕ

Не плачьте обо мне — я проживу
счастливой нищей, доброй каторжанкой,
озябшею на севере южанкой,
чахоточной да злой петербуржанкой
на малярийном юге проживу.

Не плачьте обо мне — я проживу
той хромоножкой, вышедшей на паперть,
тем пьяницей, проникнувшим на скатерть,
и этим, что малюет божью матерь,
убогим богомазом проживу.

Не плачьте обо мне — я проживу
той грамоте наученной девчонкой,
которая в грядущести нечеткой
мои стихи, моей рыжея челкой,
как дура будет знать. Я проживу.

Не плачьте обо мне — я проживу
сестры помилосердней милосердной,
в военной бесшабашности предсмертной,
да под звездой Марининой пресветлой
уж как-нибудь, а все ж я проживу.

AN INCANTATION

Don't weep for me—I'll keep going on
poor but happy, a prisoner with goodwill,
a southron frozen in the northern chill,
an evil-tempered Petersburger ill
with TB in the malarial south—I'll keep on.

Don't weep for me—I'll keep going on,
a woman limping from church as far as able,
or a drunkard who has sunken in the table,
or one who paints the Mother of God in sable,
a squalid icon-dauber—I'll keep on.

Don't weep for me—I'll keep going on
as that young girl schooled to read and write
(her bangs are red like mine) who'll know, despite
the illegibility of come what might,
all my poems without thinking. I'll keep on.

Don't weep for me—I'll keep going on,
more merciful than a sister of mercy can be
in the wild confusion of wartime agony,
and under the star of Marina the Pure and Holy
I'll somehow, somewhere, no matter what, keep on.

КЛЯНУСЬ

Тем летним снимком на крыльце чужом,
как виселица, криво и отдельно
поставленным, не приводящим в дом,
но выводящим из дому. Одета
в неистовый сатиновый доспех,
стесняющий огромный мускул горла,
так и сидишь, уже отбыв, допев
труд лошадиный голода и горя.
Тем снимком. Слабым острием локтей
ребенка с удивленною улыбкой,
которой смерть влечет к себе детей
и украшает их черты уликой.
Тяжелой болью памяти к тебе,
когда, хлебая безвоздушность горя,
от задыхания твоих тире
до крови я откашливала горло.
Присутствием твоим крала, несла,
брала себе тебя и воровала,
забыв, что ты — чужое, ты — нельзя,
ты — богово, тебя у бога мало.
Последней исхудалостию той,
добившею тебя крысиным зубом.
Благословенной родиной святой,
забывшею тебя в сиротстве грубом.
Возлюбленным тобою не к добру
вседобрым африканцем небывалым,
который созерцает детвору.
И детворою. И Тверским бульваром.
Твоим печальным отдыхом в раю,
где нет тебе ни ремесла, ни муки.
Клянусь убить Елабугу твою,
Елабугой твоей, чтоб спали внуки.

by the summer snapshot on someone else's porch
   like a gallows set crookedly and separately
   against the house, not leading in but out.
   Dressed in a furious sateen suit of armor
   squeezing the enormous muscles of your throat,
   you sit there, having done your time, having finished
   the mountainous labor of singing out hunger and grief.
by that snapshot.
               by the delicate funny bones
   of a child with a huge smile of surprise like the smile
   with which death draws children to itself and
   leaves as evidence upon their faces.
by the terrible pain of remembering you when I
   would slurp down the airlessness of grief,
   gasping for breath at all your dashes, and
   coughing to clear my throat until it bled.
   By your very existence I stole you, carried you off,
   took you over and robbed you, with never a thought
   that you belonged elsewhere—one must not touch you—
   you were God's creature—God needs you even more.
by the long and ultimate emaciation
   that, like a rat's tooth, struck the final blow.
by our sacred, blessed native land that coldly,
   callously forgot you as an orphan.
by your beloved, fantastic African,
   whose patient genius was its own ill omen
   and now contemplates the children in the park.
and by the children.
              and by Tverskoy Boulevard.
by your pathetic residence in Heaven,
   where you have no suffering—and nothing to do.
I swear to kill Elabuga, your dread
   Elabuga, that your grandchildren may sleep.

Старухи будут их стращать в ночи,
что нет ее, что нет ее, не зная:
«Спи, мальчик или девочка, молчи,
ужо придет Елабуга слепая».
О, как она всей путаницей ног
припустится ползти, так скоро, скоро.
Я опущу подкованный сапог
на щупальцы ее без приговора.
Утяжелив собой каблук, носок,
в затылок ей — и продержать подольше.
Детенышей ее зеленый сок
мне острым ядом опалит подошвы.
В хвосте ее созревшее яйцо
я брошу в землю, раз земля бездонна,
ни словом не обмолвясь про крыльцо
Марининого смертного бездомья.
И в этом я клянусь. Пока во тьме,
зловоньем ила, жабами колодца,
примеривая желтый глаз ко мне,
убить меня Елабуга клянется.

Not knowing there is no such thing, no such thing,
old women will speak spooky words at night:
"Sleep, little boy, sleep, little girl; hush, hush,
for now Elabuga the Blind draws near."
Oh, how on her whole spiderweb of legs
she quickly starts to crawl—how fast, so fast!
Without waiting for a verdict, I now bring
my hard-soled boot down on her tentacles.
I lean my weight onto my heel, then toe,
into the back of her head—as long as I can.
The green juice of the young she carries in her
eats into the leather like strong poison.
I then hurl into the earth—the fathomless earth—
the ripened egg she has carried in her tail,
but I do not broach the subject of the porch
of Marina's deathbed homelessness.
All this I swear. Meanwhile, in the dark,
stinking like slime, lurking like toads in a well,
sizing me up and down with her yellow eye,
Elabuga is swearing she will kill me.

ВАРФОЛОМЕЕВСКАЯ НОЧЬ

Я думала в уютный час дождя:
а вдруг и впрямь, по логике наитья,
заведомо безнравственно дитя,
рожденное вблизи кровопролитья.

В ту ночь, когда святой Варфоломей
на пир созвал всех алчущих, как тонок
был плач того, кто между двух огней
еще не гугенот и не католик.

Еще птенец, едва поющий вздор,
еще в ходьбе не сведущий козленок,
он выжил и присвоил первый вздох,
изъятый из дыхания казненных.

Сколь, нянюшка, ни пестуй, ни корми
дитя твое цветочным млеком меда,
в его опрятной маленькой крови
живет глоток чужого кислорода.

Он лакомка, он хочет пить еще,
не знает организм непросвещенный,
что ненасытно, сладко, горячо
вкушает дух гортани пресеченной.

Повадился дышать! Не виноват
в религиях и гибелях далеких.
И принимает он кровавый чад
за будничную выгоду для легких.

Не знаю я, в тени чьего плеча
он спит в уюте детства и злодейства.

SAINT BARTHOLOMEW'S DAY

Curled up indoors one rainy day,
I thought: going by instinct's logic,
a child born amidst a massacre
must be willfully immoral.

The night when Saint Bartholomew
convoked the faithful to his feast,
how thin between two fires a cry
not yet Huguenot or Catholic.

A fledgling still, so nonsense chanter,
a little lamb on wobbly legs,
it survived and learned to breathe
the slaughtered men and women's breath.

No matter, Nurse, how fond you are,
feed milk and honey time and again,
its tiny, tidy bloodstream carries
a mouthful of strange oxygen.

Its sweet tooth wants still more to drink:
an organism craving cate
has no idea how hotly, gladly, madly
it savors the aroma of a cut throat.

Breathing has become its habit.
It is not responsible for the faith
or death of people it does not know.
Blood in the air whets its daily breath.

I do not know beneath whose shoulder
it sleeps curled up in doing wrong,

Но и палач, и жертва палача
равно растлят незрячий сон младенца.

Когда глаза откроются — смотреть,
какой судьбою в нем взойдет отрава?
Отрадой — умертвить? Иль умереть?
Или корыстно почернеть от рабства?

Привыкшие к излишеству смертей,
вы, люди добрые, бранитесь и боритесь,
вы так бесстрашно нянчите детей,
что и детей, наверно, не боитесь.

И коль дитя расплачется со сна,
не беспокойтесь — малость виновата:
немного растревожена десна
молочными резцами вурдалака.

А если что-то глянет из ветвей,
морозом жути кожу задевая, —
не бойтесь! Это личики детей,
взлелеянных под сенью злодеянья.

Но, может быть, в беспамятстве, в раю,
тот плач звучит в честь выбора другого,
и хрупкость беззащитную свою
оплакивает маленькое горло

всем ужасом, чрезмерным для строки,
всей музыкой, не объясненной в нотах.
А в общем-то — какие пустяки!
Всего лишь — тридцать тысяч гугенотов.

but both the hangman and his victim
alike pervert its blinded dream.

So, when its eyes are open, how will
the poison in it rise? Will fate
bring joy to die, or joy to kill,
or greedily turn black, a slave?

Accustomed to so many deaths,
good people, you insult and fight,
and fearlessly raise children, too,
who never seem to frighten you.

And if a child awakens crying,
don't worry—the reason is it's young:
the baby front teeth of a vampire
are somewhat bothering its gums.

If something stares out from the branches
that turns your flesh ice-cold with fear,
don't be afraid! Those are the little faces
of children coddled in doing wrong.

But in unconsciousness, perhaps,
in heaven, that cry says something else,
and the baby throat bewails its own
unprotected brittleness

with all the terror too much for verse,
and all the song not shown by notes.
In the end, it doesn't amount to much!
Just thirty thousand Huguenots.

Есть тайна у меня от чудного цветенья,
здесь было б: чуднАГО — уместней написать.
Не зная новостей, на старый лад желтея,
цветок себе выпрашивает «ять».

Где для него возьму услад правописанья,
хоть первороден он, как речи приворот?
Что — речь, краса полей и ты, краса лесная,
как не ответный труд вобравших вас аорт?

Я этою весной все встретила растенья.
Из-под земли их ждал мой повивальный взор.
Есть тайна у меня от чудного цветенья.
И как же ей не быть? Все, что не тайна, — вздор.

Отраден первоцвет для зренья и для слуха.
— Эй, ключики! — скажи — он будет тут как тут.
Не взыщет, коль дразнить: баранчики! желтуха!
А грамотеи — чтут и буквицей зовут.

Ах, буквица моя, все твой букварь читаю.
Как азбука проста, которой невдомек,
что даже от тебя я охраняю тайну,
твой ключик золотой ее не отомкнет.

Фиалки прожила и проводила в старость
уменье медуниц изображать закат.
Черемухе моей — и той не проболталась,
под пыткой божества и под его диктант.

Уж вишня расцвела, а яблоня на завтра
оставила расцвесть... и тут же, вопреки

[THE SECRET]

I have a secret born of the wonderfullest blooming,
though *wondrous* here would be the proper word to say.
A flower, after all, never knows the news,
grows, wilts and wants to be spelled the olden way.

It is as primal as the magic spell of language,
but where will I find the way to spell delight for it?
What does speech come to, the landscape's grace and you,
    woodland beauty,
if not expression of what arteries permit?

This spring I went to greet all things both green and growing.
My midwife eye awaited their breaking through the earth.
I have a secret born of the wonderfullest blooming.
How can that not be true? Only secrets have any worth.

The primrose fills the eye and ear with easy pleasure.
"Hey, primula!" you say, and presto! it appears.
"Cowslip!" "Yellow daisy!" It does not mind your teasing,
though learned folks have called it betony for years.

Ah, betony of mine, I leaf your ABC:
how simple is the alphabet that never dreamed
that I would keep my secret from you, too—that your
gold key would not unlock whatever it may mean.

I have outlived the violets and seen the lungworts
grow senile making pictures of the setting sun.
Not a word have I let slip even to my bird cherry,
under threat of holy torture and what He ordered done.

Although the cherry is in blossom, the apple seems
to have put blooming off another day—whereat,

пустым словам, в окне, так близко и внезапно
прозрел ее цветок в конце моей строки.

Стих падает пчелой на стебли и на ветви,
чтобы цветочный мед названий целовать.
Уже не знаю я: где слово, где соцветье?
Но весь цветник земной — не гуще, чем словарь.

В отместку мне — пчела в мою строку влетела.
В чужую сласть впилась ошибка жадных уст.
Есть тайна у меня от чудного цветенья.
Но ландыш расцветет — и я проговорюсь.

despite the hollow words, a blossom opens
on my windowsill near where my verse comes to a stop.

Like a bee, that last line lands on floret, stem and tree bole
to kiss the wildflower-honeyed names. I cannot say
which is a word and which, a flower cluster. Earth's whole
flower bed is no thicker than a dictionary.

Then, in revenge, a bee flew down on what I wrote.
A greedy mouth's mistake stung someone else's sweet.
I have a secret born of the wonderfullest blooming.
When the lily of the valley blooms, I'll let it out.

СНИМОК

Улыбкой юности и славы
чуть припугнув, но не отторгнув,
от лени или для забавы
так села, как велел фотограф.

Лишь в благоденствии и лете,
при вечном детстве небосвода,
клянется ей в Оспедалетти
апрель двенадцатого года.

Сложила на коленях руки,
глядит из кружевного нимба.
И тень ее грядущей муки
защелкнута ловушкой снимка.

С тем — через «ять» — сырым и нежным
апрелем слившись воедино,
как в янтаре окаменевшем,
она пребудет невредима.

И запоздалый соглядатай
застанет на исходе века
тот профиль нежно-угловатый,
вовек сохранный в сгустке света.

Какой покой в нарядной даме,
в чьем четком облике и лике
прочесть известие о даре
так просто, как названье книги.

Кто эту горестную мету,
оттиснутую без помарок,

THE PHOTOGRAPH

Smiling nervously but brightly,
conscious of her youth and fame,
she sat the way that she was asked to
indifferently—or playing games.

Under heaven's dome's eternal childhood
April nineteen hundred twelve
has promised her in Ospedaletti
only prosperity and sun.

She looks out from a lacy nimbus,
her hands folded in her lap.
The shadow of her future torments
lies locked inside the photo's trap.

Coalesced with that sweet April—
read *Aprille*—wet and warm,
like amber that has petrified,
she will abide unharmed.

When the age comes to its end
some late-arriving sleuth will find
that tender, craggy profile preserved
forever in a clot of light.

How calm, facete the well-dressed lady
in whose clear-cut tone and look
the signs of talent show as easy
as the title of a book.

Who asked her for a present of
this doleful commentary framed

и этот лоб, и челку эту
себе выпрашивал в подарок?

Что ей самой в ее портрете?
Пожмет плечами: как угодно!
И выведет: Оспедалетти.
Апрель двенадцатого года.

Как на земле свежо и рано!
Грядущий день, дай ей отсрочку!
Пускай она допишет: «Анна
Ахматова», — и капнет точку.

on paper without a pencil mark,
this forehead, and this fringe of bangs?

What's in her portrait for herself?
She gives a shrug: please yourselves!
And paints a picture—Ospedaletti,
April nineteen hundred twelve.

How fresh, still early here on earth!
O morrow, let her have more time!
Wait until she's done, signs "Anna
Akhmatova" on the last line.

ДАЧНЫЙ РОМАН

Вот вам роман из жизни дачной.
Он начинался в октябре,
когда зимы кристалл невзрачный
мерцал при утренней заре.
И тот, столь счастливо любивший
печаль и блеск осенних дней,
был зренья моего добычей
и пленником души моей.

Недавно, добрый и почтенный,
сосед мой умер, и вдова,
для совершенья жизни бренной,
уехала, а дом сдала.
Так появились брат с сестрою.
По вечерам в чужом окне
сияла кроткою звездою
их жизнь, неведомая мне.

В благовоспитанном соседстве
поврозь мы дождались зимы,
но, с тайным любопытством в сердце,
невольно сообщались мы.
Когда вблизи моей тетради
встречались солнце и сосна,
тропинкой, скрытой в снегопаде,
спешила к станции сестра.
Я полюбила тратить зренье
на этот мимолетный бег,
и длилась целое мгновенье
улыбка, свежая, как снег.

Брат был свободен и не должен
вставать, пока не встанет день.

A SUMMER-HOUSE LOVE STORY

Here's a summer-house love story for you.
It all began one October when
an unassuming crystal of winter
glittered in the morning sun,
and he who had been so happily fond of
the shining sorrow of autumn days
was bagged by my eyesight as being fair game
and imprisoned in my spirit's ways.

My kind and honorable neighbor
died recently, and then his spouse
(to pull her remaining life together)
left and rented out the house.
Enter then the brother and sister.
Their life that I knew nothing about
twinkled like a faint star cluster
in their alien window every night.

With perfect, neighborly politeness
we kept apart, awaiting winter,
but secretly so inquisitive
that each responded to the other:
when the sun cast shadows through the pine
not far from where my notebook lay,
she would rush down to the station,
her path half-lost in falling snow.
I loved to spend my time observing
this all-too-short-and-sudden flight,
and for an instant I would smile
a smile as fresh and bright as snow.

The brother seemed a professional man—
he got up only after dawn—

«Кто он? — я думала. — Художник?»
А думать дальше было лень.
Всю зиму я жила привычкой
их лица видеть поутру
и знать, с какою электричкой
брат пустится встречать сестру.
Я наблюдала их проказы,
снежки, огни, когда темно,
и знала, что они прекрасны,
а кто они — не все ль равно?
Я вглядывалась в них так остро,
как в глушь иноязычных книг,
и слаще явного знакомства
мне были вымыслы о них.
Их дней цветущие картины
растила я меж сонных век,
сослав их образы в куртины,
в заглохший сад, в старинный снег.

Весной мы сблизились — не тесно,
не участив случайность встреч.
Их лица были так чудесно
ясны, так благородна речь.
Мы сиживали в час заката
в саду, где липа и скамья.
Брат без сестры, сестра без брата,
как ими любовалась я!
Я шла домой и до рассвета
зрачок держала на луне.
Когда бы не несчастье это,
была б несчастна я вполне.

Тек август. Двум моим соседям
прискучила его жара.
Пришли, и молвил брат: — Мы едем.

"What's he?" I wondered; "perhaps a painter?"
but was too lazy to think on.
All winter I became accustomed
to seeing their faces every morning,
to know at which commuter train
the two of them would meet again.
I kept an eye on how they frolicked—
their snowball fights, the house lit up
and in the dark—two lovely people—
but who they were—does it really matter?
I stared at them as keenly as
into books in foreign languages;
much sweeter than a budding friendship
were all the fancies I made up.
Falling off in the land of Nod,
imagining them in a flower bed
or a tangled garden or long-gone snow,
I pictured all their days in bloom.

In spring we started growing close—
not too—met once or twice by chance.
Their faces were so very bright;
the way they spoke was very noble.
As the sun was setting, we used to sit
on the garden bench beneath the linden.
At him alone, at her without her brother—
how I loved to look at them!
And then I would go home and stare
wide-eyed at the moon till dawn.
If not for such unhappiness
I would have been a soul forlorn.

August passed. My two neighbors
found they couldn't stand the heat.
They came over. The brother said, "We're going."

— Мы едем, — молвила сестра.
Простились мы — скорей степенно,
чем пылко. Выпили вина.
Они уехали. Стемнело.
Их ключ остался у меня.

Затем пришло письмо от брата:
«Коли прогневаетесь Вы,
я не страшусь: мне нет возврата
в соседство с Вами, в дом вдовы.
Зачем, простак недальновидный,
я тронул на снегу Ваш след?
Как будто фосфор ядовитый
в меня вселился — еле видный,
доныне излучает свет
ладонь...» — с печалью деловитой
я поняла, что он — поэт,
и заскучала...
Тем не мене
отвыкшие скрипеть ступени
я поступью моей бужу,
когда в соседний дом хожу,
одна играю в свет и тени
и для таинственной затеи
часы зачем-то завожу
и долго за полночь сижу.
Ни брата, ни сестры. Лишь в скрипе
зайдется ставня. Видно мне,
как ум забытой ими книги
печально светится во тьме.
Уж осень. Разве осень? Осень.
Вот свет. Вот сумерки легли.
— Но где ж роман? — читатель спросит. —
Здесь нет героя, нет любви!
...

("We're going," the sister's voice repeats.)
We said good-bye—more formally
than fondly. Drank a glass of wine.
They left. The darkness came down slowly.
The house key stayed behind with me.

Then came a letter from the brother:
"Although I may arouse your wrath,
I do not fear to say that never
can I be your neighbor in the widow's house.
Oh, why—shortsighted fool—did I ever
trod where you tread that snowy path?
As if some toxic phosphorus
had gotten into me, scarce seen,
and now my palm emits its light . . ."
In sorrow born of common sense
I realized he was a poet—and I—
I had been yearning . . .
Nevertheless
by treading them each time I enter
the house next door, I wake the steps
no longer used to creaks and squeaks;
alone I thread through light and shadow,
and for something secretive to do
I wind the clock, then sit beside it
to all hours of the night.
No brother, no sister. Only the shutter
makes a screech. I can see
how the concept of their forgotten book
shines sadly in the dark.
Fall already. Really? Fall.
There's the light. And there's the dusk.
"But where's the story?" the reader asks.
"This has no hero and no love!"
...

Меж тем — все есть! Окрест крепчает
октябрь, и это означает,
что тот, столь счастливо любивший
печаль и блеск осенних дней,
идет дорогою обычной
на жадный зов свечи моей.
Сад облетает первобытный,
и от любви кровопролитной
немеет сердце, и в костры
сгребают листья... Брат сестры,
прощай навеки! Ночью лунной
другой возлюбленный безумный,
чья поступь молодому льду
не тяжела, минует тьму
и к моему подходит дому.
Уж если говорить: люблю! —
то, разумеется, ему,
а не кому-нибудь другому.

Очнись, читатель любопытный!
Вскричи: — Как, намертво убитый
и прочный, точно лунный свет,
тебя он любит?! —
Вовсе нет.
Хочу соврать и не совру,
как ни мучительна мне правда.
Боюсь, что он влюблен в сестру
стихи слагающего брата.
Я влюблена, она любима,
вот вам сюжета грозный крен.
Ах, я не зря ее ловила
на робком сходстве с Анной Керн!
В час грустных наших посиделок
твержу ему: — Тебя злодей

Wait! It has it all! October
grips the countryside; that means
that he who had been so happily fond of
the shining sorrow of autumn days
is coming along the usual path
to the greedy summons my candle makes.
The primeval garden is turning bare;
the heart grows numb from all the blood-
stained love; huge piles of fallen leaves
are being burned . . . Sister's brother,
farewell forever! Some moonlit night
another half-mad lover might
(if he's not too heavy for the ice
just formed and can get through the dark)
make his way up to my house.
And if I'm going to say, "I love you!"
why, naturally, it'll be to him
and not to somebody or other.

Wake up, inquisitive reader! "What, dead?"—
shout it—"What, stiff, stark dead
and no more solid than moonlight and just as pale,
he loves you?!"
Not a bit.
I want to cheat, but I won't do it
no matter how the truth may hurt.
I'm afraid he fell in love with the sister
of the brother who composed the verse.
I'm in love, and she's beloved—
now that's a plot with a heavy turn.
Oh, certainly I knew that she
resembled Pushkin's Anna Kern.
So, when we sit around on lonely
evenings, I tell him squarely. "Some villain

убил! Ты заново содеян
из жизни, из любви моей!
Коль ты таков — во мглу веков
назад сошлю!
Не отвечает
и думает: — Она стихов
не пишет часом? — и скучает.

Вот так, столетия подряд,
все влюблены мы невпопад,
и странствуют, не совпадая,
два сердца, сирых две ладьи,
ямб ненасытный услаждая
великой горечью любви.

killed you! You've been created anew
from life, out of my love for you!
But if that's what you're like, I'll send you back
into the gloom of time."
No response from him,
who ponders: "She doesn't happen
to write poems, does she?" And his spirit slackens.

Still, after centuries, just like that,
we fall in love at the drop of a hat,
and hearts keep circling in their flight,
like vessels passing in the night,
sweetening verse with samples of
the true and bitter taste of love.

Стихотворения чудный театр,
нежься и кутайся в бархат дремотный.
Я ни при чем, это занят работой
чуждых божеств несравненный талант.

Я лишь простак, что извне приглашен
для сотворенья стороннего действа.
Я не хочу! Но меж звездами где-то
грозную палочку взял дирижер.

Стихотворения чудный театр,
нам ли решать, что сегодня сыграем?
Глух к наставленьям и недосягаем
в музыку нашу влюбленный тиран.

Что он диктует? И есть ли навес —
нас упасти от любви его лютой?
Как помыкает безграмотной лютней
безукоризненный гений небес!

Стихотворения чудный театр,
некого спрашивать: вместо ответа —
мука, когда раздирают отверстья
труб — для рыданья и губ — для тирад.

Кончено! Лампы огня не таят.
Вольно! Прощаюсь с божественным игом.
Вкратце — всей жизнью и смертью — разыгран
стихотворения чудный театр.

O magic theater of a poem,
spoil yourself, wrap up in sleepy velvet.
I don't matter. A matchless talent
is busy here with otherworldly gods.

I'm just a Simple Simon that got asked
to put a morality play together.
Oh no! I cried, but somewhere up in heaven
the conductor lifted his threatening baton.

O magic theater of a poem,
do we decide what will be on the playbill?
A tyrant mad with love hears no instructions,
cannot respond to music that we make.

What does he dictate? And is the curtain there
to save us from his fierce, unbridled passion?
Heaven's pure, uncriticizable genius
commands by means of an illiterate lute!

O magic theater of a poem,
there's no one here to ask: instead of answers
there's only pain when they rip the flues of failure
to let out tears, or lips to launch a speech.

The end! The footlights are no longer on.
At ease! I say farewell to heaven's burden.
Briefly, all life and death has been played out in
the magic theater of a poem.

СКАЗКА О ДОЖДЕ

в нескольких эпизодах
с диалогом и хором детей

Е. ЕВТУШЕНКО

1.

Со мной с утра не расставался Дождь.
— О, отвяжись! — я говорила грубо.
Он отступал, но преданно и грустно
вновь шел за мной, как маленькая дочь.

Дождь, как крыло, прирос к моей спине.
Его корила я:
— Стыдись, негодник!
К тебе в слезах взывает огородник!
Иди к цветам!
Что ты нашел во мне?

Меж тем вокруг стоял суровый зной.
Дождь был со мной, забыв про все на свете.
Вокруг меня приплясывали дети,
как около машины поливной.

Я, с хитростью в душе, вошла в кафе.
Я спряталась за стол, укрытый нишей.
Дождь за окном пристроился, как нищий,
и сквозь стекло желал пройти ко мне.

Я вышла. И была моя щека
наказана пощечиною влаги,

A FAIRY TALE ABOUT RAIN

In Several Episodes with
Dialogue and Children's Chorus

FOR Y. YEVTUSHENKO

1.

From morning on, Rain wouldn't leave my side.
"Go away! Get lost!" I kept repeating rudely.
It would drop back, then once more follow sadly
and devotedly like a little child.

Rain, like a wing, took root upon my back.
I scolded it:
                    "Shame on you, you bum!
A gardener's shedding tears for you to come!
Go to the flowers!
                    You think it's you I lack?"

Everything was wilting in the scorching heat:
but oblivious Rain was out for a walk with me.
Children hopped and skipped as if around
a water truck wetting down a street.

Then, thinking I was clever, I went into
a café and hid in a niche behind a table.
Outside the window Rain stood like a beggar
making signs to me it wanted to come in.

Out I went. And what do I get but a slap
of moisture on my cheek! Feeling sorry

но тут же Дождь, в печали и отваге,
омыл мне губы запахом щенка.

Я думаю, что вид мой стал смешон.
Сырым платком я шею обвязала.
Дождь на моем плече, как обезьяна,
сидел.
И город этим был смущен.

Обрадованный слабостью моей,
он детским пальцем щекотал мне ухо.
Сгущалась засуха. Все было сухо.
И только я промокла до костей.

2.

Но я была в тот дом приглашена,
где строго ждали моего привета,
где над янтарным озером паркета
всходила люстры чистая луна.

Я думала: что делать мне с Дождем?
Ведь он со мной расстаться не захочет.
Он наследит там. Он ковры замочит.
Да с ним меня вообще не пустят в дом.

Я строго объяснила: — Доброта
во мне сильна, но все ж не безгранична.
Тебе ходить со мною неприлично. —
Дождь на меня смотрел, как сирота.

— Ну, черт с тобой, — решила я, — иди!
Какой любовью на меня ты пролит?

but also bolder, and smelling like a puppy
Rain then licked and laved my lips.

I think I must have looked ridiculous:
around my neck I tied a soaking wet
scarf. Rain sat on my shoulder like a pet
monkey. The whole town was embarrassed for us.

Delighted to have found me weak as sin,
Rain tickled my ear with a childlike finger.
The drought got worse. Everything turned ginger.
I alone was soaked through to the skin.

2.

But I had been invited to a home
where people waited to give me formal welcome,
where above the amber lake of the parquet flooring
a chandelier rose as clearly as the moon.

I thought and thought, What can I do with Rain?
Obviously, it's not about to leave.
It'll track the floor. It'll soak the rugs.
If I bring it along, they'll never let me in.

I made things very clear: "My kindness goes
a long way, but all the same it has a limit.
For you to be taking a walk with me is indecent."
Rain looked at me with two big orphan eyes.

"Oh, damn you! The hell with it! Come on!" I said.
"But why have you been poured on me? From fondness?

Ах, этот странный климат, будь он проклят! —
Прощенный Дождь запрыгал впереди.

3.

Хозяин дома оказал мне честь,
которой я не стоила. Однако,
промокшая всей шкурой, как ондатра,
я у дверей звонила ровно в шесть.

Дождь, притаившись за моей спиной,
дышал в затылок жалко и щекотно.
Шаги — глазок — молчание — щеколда.
Я извинилась: — Этот Дождь со мной.

Позвольте, он побудет на крыльце?
Он слишком влажный, слишком удлиненный
для комнат.
— Вот как? — молвил удивленный
хозяин, изменившийся в лице.

4.

Признаться, я любила этот дом.
В нем свой балет всегда вершила легкость.
О, здесь углы не ушибают локоть,
здесь палец не порежется ножом.

Любила все: как медленно хрустят
шелка хозяйки, затененной шарфом,
и, более всего, плененный шкафом —
мою царевну спящую — хрусталь.

The climate's strange, I guess; well, curses on it!"
Forgiven, Rain set out skipping on ahead.

3.

Honored to be invited (but in a fix),
I felt I was unworthy. In spite of that,
dripping wet all over like a muskrat,
I rang the front door bell exactly at six.

Rain, half hiding up and down my spine,
was tickling, breathing morosely down my neck.
First, steps—the peephole—silence—then the latch:
I apologized at once: "This Rain is mine.

Excuse me, may it stay on the porch perhaps?
It's much too wet and much too long, strung out
for any room."
                    His face completely changed,
quoth my poor, astonished host, "How's that?"

4.

I really liked that house, I must admit.
There easy lightness danced its own ballet.
No corners bruised your elbow on your way;
no finger worried about knives cutting it.

I loved everything: the susurrous, slow silks
my hostess wore, her face shaded by a shawl,
and, imprisoned in a cupboard on the wall,
my favorite, my sleeping princess—cut glass.

Тот, в семь румянцев розовевший спектр,
в гробу стеклянном, мертвый и прелестный.
Но я очнулась. Ритуал приветствий,
как опера, станцован был и спет.

5.

Хозяйка дома, честно говоря,
меня бы не любила непременно,
но робость поступить несовременно
чуть-чуть мешала ей, что было зря.

— Как поживаете? (О блеск грозы,
смиренный в тонком горлышке гордячки!)
— Благодарю, — сказала я, — в горячке
я провалялась, как свинья в грязи.

(Со мной творилось что-то в этот раз.
Ведь я хотела, поклонившись слабо,
сказать:
— Живу хоть суетно, но славно,
тем более, что снова вижу вас.)

Она произнесла:
— Я вас браню.
Помилуйте, такая одаренность!
Сквозь дождь! И расстоянья отдаленность! —
Вскричали все:
— К огню ее, к огню!

— Когда-нибудь, во времени другом,
на площади, средь музыки и брани,
мы б свидеться могли при барабане,

It lay, a rosy spectrum of seven shades
of blush, dead and lovely in its glassy grave.
But I stopped dreaming: the greeting ritual,
like an opera, was waltzed out, sung, replayed.

5.

The lady of the house, to tell the truth,
certainly wouldn't have shown me any liking
if she hadn't been leery of being thought unmodern,
which, though pointless, kept her from being uncouth.

"How do you do?" (O lightning bolt subdued
in one overbearing woman's slender throat!)
"Thanks, fine," I said, "though in my crazy hurry
I've been wallowing about, like a pig in mud."

(Something was happening to me that time.
Of course I meant to say, after making a little
bow:
        "Not doing much of anything,
but things are great, especially being here again.")

She then declared:
                "I have a bone to pick.
For heaven's sake, you're so very talented!
Out in the rain! And such a dreadful distance!"
So everyone then shouted:
                        "To the fire! Quick!"

"Some other time, in some age that has gone by,
in some square filled with music and with shouting,
we might have met to the sound of some drum beating,

вскричали б вы:
— В огонь ее, в огонь!

За все! За дождь! За после! За тогда!
За чернокнижье двух зрачков чернейших,
за звуки, с губ, как косточки черешни,
летящие без всякого труда!

Привет тебе! Нацель в меня прыжок.
Огонь, мой брат, мой пес многоязыкий!
Лижи мне руки в нежности великой!
Ты — тоже Дождь! Как влажен твой ожог!

— Ваш несколько причудлив монолог, —
проговорил хозяин уязвленный. —
Но, впрочем, слава поросли зеленой!
Есть прелесть в поколенье молодом.

— Не слушайте меня! Ведь я в бреду! —
просила я. — Все это Дождь наделал.
Он целый день меня казнил, как демон.
Да, это Дождь вовлек меня в беду.

И вдруг я увидала — там, в окне,
мой верный Дождь один стоял и плакал.
В моих глазах двумя слезами плавал
лишь след его, оставшийся во мне.

6.

Одна из гостий, протянув бокал,
туманная, как голубь над карнизом,

and you'd have cried:
                              'Into the fire! Alive!

'For everything! For Rain! For afterward!
For then! For the black magic of a pair
of the blackest eyes! For sounds flying through air
like bird-cherry pits from lips not caring where!

'Hail to thee! Take me with a leap.
Fire, my brother, my many-tongued hound!
Now lick my hands in wondrous tenderness!
You, too, are Rain! How wet the burns you keep!' "

"Your monologue is somewhat whimsical,"
my wounded host allowed himself to say.
"But nevertheless, praise be to new green shoots!
The younger generation's charm is mystical."

"Pay no attention! I'm lost in foggy bubbles!"
I humbly begged. "You know it's all Rain's fault.
It spent the whole day like a demon punishing me.
In fact, 'twas Rain that led me into trouble."

And suddenly I noticed that my faithful Rain
was standing all alone outside the window
crying. Two huge tears welled up in my eyes,
the only trace that it had left behind.

6.

Holding out her wineglass, a lady guest,
as spacey as a pigeon on a cornice,

спросила с неприязнью и капризом:
— Скажите, правда, что ваш муж богат?

— Богат ли он? Не знаю. Не вполне.
Но он богат. Ему легка работа.
Хотите знать один секрет? — Есть что-то
неизлечимо нищее во мне.

Его я научила колдовству —
во мне была такая откровенность —
он разом обратит любую ценность
в круг на воде, в зверька или траву.

Я докажу вам! Дайте мне кольцо.
Спасем звезду из тесноты колечка! —
Она кольца мне не дала, конечно,
в недоуменье отстранив лицо.

— И, знаете, еще одна деталь —
меня влечет подохнуть под забором.
(Язык мой так и воспалялся вздором.
О, это Дождь твердил мне свой диктант.)

7.

Все, Дождь, тебе припомнится потом!
Другая гостья, голосом глубоким,
осведомилась:
— Одаренных богом
кто одаряет? И каким путем?

Как погремушкой, мной гремел озноб:
— Приходит бог, преласков и превесел,

feeling hostile to me and capricious,
asked:
          "Is your husband really rich?"

"Is he? I've no idea. Not really. But
somewhat. He is. Work's easy for him. Would you like
to know a secret? There's something here inside
that keeps me irreparably destitute.

"I taught him magic things and witches' craft"
(that's how candidly I talked then),
"so he can in a trice make any gem
a floating circle, a little beast, or grass.

"I'll show you how. Let me have your ring.
We'll save that star from squeezing in its setting!"
Of course she didn't give it to me; letting
me know her bewilderment, she turned away.

"And one more little thing I'd add today:
I'd like to kick the bucket beneath a fence."
(My tongue, it seemed, had become inflamed with nonsense.
O that was Rain dictating what to say.)

                    7.

You'll later recollect it all, dear Rain!
Another lady guest with a bass voice
inquired:
          "Who gives presents to the ones
God has endowed? And how would it be done?"

A shudder, like a rattle, shook me in place:
"God comes, so very cheerful, very gentle,

немножко старомоден, как профессор,
и милостью ваш осеняет лоб.

А далее — летите вверх и вниз,
в кровь разбивая локти и коленки
о снег, о воздух, об углы Кваренги,
о простыни гостиниц и больниц.

Василия Блаженного, в зубцах,
тот острый купол помните?
                    Представьте —
всей кожей об него!
— Да вы присядьте! —
она меня одернула в сердцах.

8.

Тем временем, для радости гостей,
творилось что-то новое, родное:
в гостиную впускали кружевное,
серебряное облако детей.

Хозяюшка, прости меня, я зла!
Я все лгала, я поступала дурно!
В тебе, как на губах у стеклодува,
явился выдох чистого стекла.

Душой твоей насыщенный сосуд,
дитя твое, отлитое так нежно!
Как точен контур, обводящий нечто!
О том не знала я, не обессудь.

Хозяюшка, звериный гений твой
в отчаянье вседенном и всенощном

somewhat old-fashioned, a typical professor,
and overlays your forehead with His grace.

"And furthermore—fly high, fly low, beat, beat
your elbows and your pretty knees to pieces
on the snow, the air, Quarenghi's cornices,
on hospital and hotel cotton sheets.

"You know the Blessed Vassily, the battlements,
that very pointed steeple, remember? Just think:
you could scrape your whole skin off!"
                                    "Sit down, you fink!"
She yanked me down in furious nettlement.

8.

In the meantime, for the pleasure of the guests,
something new but quite familial was arranged:
a lacy, silver cloud of children came
pouring into that formal living room.

Forgive me, hostess mine, my dear, I'm bad!
I fibbed so much, made myself look foolish!
From you, as from the lips of a glassblower,
there came an exhalation of pure glass.

A lovely vessel that your soul enriched,
this child of yours so fondly, gently molded!
How clear the outline whatever it's enfolding!
I had no idea. Please don't take that amiss.

O hostess mine, your genius like a beast
in desperation the livelong day and night

над детищем твоим, о, над сыночком
великой поникает головой.

Дождь мои губы звал к ее руке.
Я плакала:
— Прости меня! Прости же!
Глаза твои премудры и пречисты!

9.

Тут хор детей возник невдалеке:
Наш номер был объявлен.
Уста младенцев. Жуть.
Мы — яблочки от яблонь.
Вот наша месть и суть.

Вниманье! Детский лепет.
Мы вас не подведем.
Не зря великолепен
камин, согревший дом.

В лопатках — холод милый
и острия двух крыл.
Нам кожу алюминий,
как изморозь, покрыл.

Чтоб было жить не скучно,
нас трогает порой
искусствочко, искусство,
ребеночек чужой.

Дождливость есть оплошность
пустых небес. Ура!

is hanging its enormous head above
your great creation, this small
son from your breast.

Rain bent my lips down toward her hand.
I wept:
        "Forgive me! Forgive me, please!
Your eyes are clear and pure and very wise!"

9.

A children's chorus started up nearby:
    Our number was announced.
    The mouths of babes. The awe.
    We're the apples on the trees.
    That's what we're all about.

Look out! Kiddy babble.
We won't put you on the spot.
There's a reason fire's able
to keep houses piping hot.
Shoulder blades' sweet cold
meets the sharpness of two wings.
Aluminum, like hoarfrost,
has covered up our skins.

So things don't get too dull
we sometimes find our lid
blown off by artsy-fartsy stuff,
or art, or someone's kid.

A lot of rain's a blunder
by empty skies. Hurrah!

О пошлость, ты не подлость,
ты лишь уют ума.

От боли и от гнева
ты нас спасешь потом.
Целуем, королева,
твой бархатный подол!

10.

Лень, как болезнь, во мне смыкала круг.
Мое плечо вело чужую руку.
Я, как птенца, в ладони грела рюмку.
Попискивал ее открытый клюв.

Хозяюшка, вы ощущали грусть
над мальчиком, заснувшим спозаранку,
в уста его, в ту алчущую ранку,
отравленную проливая грудь?

Вдруг в нем, как в перламутровом яйце,
спала пружина музыки согбенной?
Как радуга — в бутоне краски белой?
Как тайный мускул красоты — в лице?

Как в Сашеньке — непробужденный Блок?
Медведица, вы для какой забавы
в детеныше влюбленными зубами
выщелкивали бога, словно блох?

Banality's not under-
handed: it's Mind gone blah.

From pain and, also, anger
you'll save us now and then.
So, Queen, Your Royal Highness,
we kiss your velvet hem!

10.

Torpor like an illness closed me round.
Some stranger's arms seemed hanging from my shoulders.
I warmed a wineglass in my hand like a baby
bird; the open beak made a chirping sound.

O hostess mine, did you ever feel grief
to see your son asleep in the early morning
while over him you were pouring your poisoned
breast into his craving wound, his mouth?

Was suddenly there asleep in him, as in
a pearly egg, a spring of coiled-up music?
As in a bud of white oil paint, a rainbow?
Like beauty's secret muscle in a face?

As in little Sasha slept great Blok to be?
She-bear here and in the sky, what pleasure
did you get by combing God from your cub's fur
with your fond teeth and cracking Him like a flea?

11.

Хозяйка налила мне коньяка:
— Вас лихорадит. Грейтесь у камина. —
Прощай, мой Дождь!
Как весело, как мило
принять мороз на кончик языка!

Как крепко пахнет розой от вина!
Вино, лишь ты ни в чем не виновато.
Во мне расщеплен атом винограда,
во мне горит двух разных роз война.

Вино мое, я твой заблудший князь,
привязанный к двум деревам склоненным.
Разъединяй! Не бойся же! Со звоном
меня со мной пусть разлучает казнь!

Я делаюсь все больше, все добрей!
Смотрите — я уже добра, как клоун,
вам в ноги опрокинутый поклоном!
Уж тесно мне средь окон и дверей!

О господи, какая доброта!
Скорей! Жалеть до слез! Пасть на колени!
Я вас люблю! Застенчивость калеки
бледнит мне щеки и кривит уста.

Что делать мне для вас хотя бы раз?
Обидьте! Не жалейте, обижая!
Вот кожа моя — голая, большая:
как холст для красок, чист простор для ран!

Я вас люблю без меры и стыда!
Как небеса, круглы мои объятья.

11.

My hostess filled my glass with cognac, said:
"You're feverish. Warm up by the fire."
Farewell, my Rain!
     How cheering, how much desired
to feel the freezing cold now with my tongue!

How much the liquor smells of roses! Or
whatever; it alone is not at fault.
In me the atom of the grape is split;
in me there burns two different roses' war.

Sweet wine, I am your lost and wandering prince,
bound hand and foot to two bent-over trees.
Let go! Don't be afraid! Let execution
ring to cut me from the I I was!

I'm getting bigger, bigger, better too!
Why, look—I'm just as kind as any clown
trying to bow before you upside down!
These doors and windows hold me tight like screws!

O Lord, what kindness speaks! what goodness here!
Come quick! Now moved to tears! Now on my knees!
I love you! Only a cripple's shyness keeps
my poor cheeks pale and twists my humble lips.

What can I do for you, though only once?
Hurt me now! Don't hold back the hurting!
See my skin: it's naked and enormous;
for paints, a canvas; for wounds, a clear expanse.

I love you without measure, without shame!
My arms embrace you roundly like the heavens.

Мы из одной купели. Все мы братья.
Мой мальчик, Дождь! Скорей иди сюда!

12.

Прошел по спинам быстрый холодок.
В тиши раздался страшный крик хозяйки.
И ржавые, оранжевые знаки
вдруг выплыли на белый потолок.

И — хлынул Дождь! Его ловили в таз.
В него впивались веники и щетки.
Он вырывался. Он летел на щеки,
прозрачной слепотой вставал у глаз.

Отплясывал нечаянный канкан.
Звенел, играя с хрусталем воскресшим.
Дом над Дождем уж замыкал свой скрежет,
как мышцы обрывающий капкан.

Дождь с выраженьем ласки и тоски,
паркет марая, полз ко мне на брюхе.
В него мужчины, поднимая брюки,
примерившись, вбивали каблуки.

Его скрутили тряпкой половой
и выжимали, брезгуя, в уборной.
Гортанью, вдруг охрипшей и убогой,
кричала я:
        — Не трогайте! Он мой!

Он был живой, как зверь или дитя.
О, вашим детям жить в беде и муке!

We shared a common font. We all are brethren.
Come quick! Come to me quick, my sweet boy, Rain!

12.

A sudden shudder went down every back.
The hostess's frightened scream rang through the silence.
And rusty-colored orange marks, or omens,
swam suddenly across the ceiling's cracks.

Rain poured down! They caught it in a bowl.
Their brooms and brushes pricked it, stung it, but tearing
itself away, it flew in people's faces
and rose in limpid blindness in their eyes.

Unexpectedly kicking up its heels,
it rang out on the resurrected crystal.
Overhead the house—like a trap disjoining muscle—
was slowly drawing shut its jaws of steel.

Kindness and longing in its face, then Rain.
as it wet the floor, crawled to me on its belly.
Grown men, thinking to do something, lifted
their trouser legs and stomped it again and again.

They surrounded it with floor rags, mopped it dry,
then squeezed them out fastidiously in the toilet.
My throat now suddenly hoarse and feeling wretched,
"Don't you dare touch that! It's mine!"
                                   I cried.

It was alive, like some wild beast or child.
O may your children now know toil and trouble!

Слепые, тайн не знающие руки
зачем вы окунули в кровь Дождя?

Хозяин дома прошептал:
— Учти,
еще ответишь ты за эту встречу! —
Я засмеялась:
— Знаю, что отвечу.
Вы безобразны. Дайте мне пройти.

13.

Пугал прохожих вид моей беды.
Я говорила:
— Ничего. Оставьте.
Пройдет и это. —
На сухом асфальте
я целовала пятнышко воды.

Земли перекалялась нагота,
и горизонт вкруг города был розов.
Повергнутое в страх Бюро прогнозов
осадков не сулило никогда.

You with hands that know no mystery,
blind people, why did you plunge them in Rain's blood?

The house's master whispered:
                              "Don't forget,
someday you'll have to answer for this evening!"
I burst out laughing:
                              "Indeed, I know I will.
You're outrageous, all of you. Now let me out."

13.

My sad expression frightened passersby.
I said to them:
                              "It doesn't matter. Don't worry.
Things'll soon be better."
                              On the hard macadam surface
I kissed a speck of water as it dried.

Earth's nudeness overheated—the mercury soared—
and the horizon was pink all around the city.
Terrified, the weather bureau forecast
no precipitation forevermore.

ОЗНОБ

Хвораю, что ли, — третий день дрожу,
как лошадь, ожидающая бега.
Надменный мой сосед по этажу
и тот вскричал:
— Как вы дрожите, Белла!

Но образумьтесь! Странный ваш недуг
колеблет стены и сквозит повсюду.
Моих детей он воспаляет дух
и по ночам звонит в мою посуду.

Ему я отвечала:
— Я дрожу
все более — без умысла худого.
А впрочем, передайте этажу,
что вечером я ухожу из дома.

Но этот трепет так меня трепал,
в мои слова вставлял свои ошибки,
моей ногой приплясывал, мешал
губам соединиться для улыбки.

Сосед мой, перевесившись в пролет,
следил за мной брезгливо, но без фальши.
Его я обнадежила:
— Пролог
вы наблюдали. Что-то будет дальше?

Моей болезни не скучал сюжет!
В себе я различала, взглядом скорбным,
мельканье диких и чужих существ,
как в капельке воды под микроскопом.
...

CHILLS

I guess I'm sick, because this is the third day
I've been shivering like a horse waiting for the start,
Even my snobbish neighbor on the floor
keeps shouting: "Bella, you're practically shaking yourself
   apart!

"Pull yourself together! Your weird disease
makes the walls tremble and blows through all the cracks.
It gives my kids inflammation of the feelings
and rattles the dishes drying in the rack."

And so I'd say to him:
               "I'm shivering
more and more—without malice prepense.
But by the way, tell everyone on the floor
that this evening I'm quitting our residence."

But the general unease rendered me so queasy
that I kept making stupid verbal slips,
one leg began to hop, and I couldn't even
get a smile to form upon my lips.

Leaning over in the stairwell, my neighbor
eyed me squeamishly and kept away.
I buoyed him up:
           "You watched the introduction.
What do you suppose will happen today?"

The plot my sickness followed wasn't boring!
With one sad glance, I could see inside
me strange and savage creatures glimmering
as in a water drop on a laboratory slide.
...

Все тяжелей меня хлестала дрожь,
вбивала в кожу острые гвоздочки.
Так по осине ударяет дождь,
наказывая все ее листочки.

Я думала: как быстро я стою!
Прочь мускулы несутся и резвятся!
Мое же тело, свергнув власть мою,
ведет себя свободно и развязно.

Оно все дальше от меня! А вдруг
оно исчезнет вольно и опасно,
как ускользает шар из детских рук
и ниточку разматывает с пальца?

Все это мне не нравилось.
Врачу
сказала я, хоть перед ним робела:
— Я, знаете, горда и не хочу
сносить и впредь непослушанье тела.

Врач объяснил:
— Ваша болезнь проста.
Она была б и вовсе безобидна,
но ваших колебаний частота
препятствует осмотру — вас не видно.

Вот так, когда вибрирует предмет
и велика его движений малость,
он зрительно почти сведен на нет
и выглядит, как слабая туманность.

Врач подключил свой золотой прибор
к моим предметам неопределенным,

The shivering lashed me ever more painfully,
driving its sharp tacks into my soft skin,
as rain strikes hard upon an aspen, punishing
each quivering leaf again and again.

I kept thinking: how rapidly I'm standing!
My muscles are running and jumping playfully!
Having dethroned my power, my body's behaving
openly, familiarly and free.

And going farther, dangerously away from me.
Will it one day decide to leave without a sound,
the way a balloon slips from a young child's hands
and string around his finger comes unwound?

I didn't like how things were going. And so
I told the doctor, despite my reticence:
"I have some self-respect, you see, and can't
forever take my body's disobedience."

The doctor then explained: "It's very simple.
Your harmless illness might even be derisible
if the frequency of oscillations preventing
examination didn't render you invisible.

"You see, when an object's in vibration
and the smallness of its movements is very great,
to the naked eye it shrinks to almost nothing
and appears like distant, blurry haze."

The doctor connected his golden apparatus
to all my indeterminate, vague parts,

и острый электрический прибой
охолодил меня огнем зеленым.

И ужаснулась стрелка и шкала!
Взыграла ртуть в неистовом подскоке!
Последовал предсмертный всплеск стекла,
и кровь из пальцев высекли осколки.

Встревожься, добрый доктор, оглянись!
Но он, не озадаченный нимало,
провозгласил:
— Ваш бедный организм
сейчас функционирует нормально.

Мне стало грустно. Знала я сама
свою причастность к этой высшей норме.
Не умещаясь в узости ума,
плыл надо мной ее чрезмерный номер.

И, многозначной цифрою мытарств
наученная, нервная система,
пробившись, как пружины сквозь матрац,
рвала мне кожу и вокруг свистела.

Уродующий кисть огромный пульс
всегда гудел, всегда хотел на волю.
В конце концов казалось: к черту! Пусть
им захлебнусь, как Петербург Невою!

А по ночам — мозг навострится, ждет.
Слух так открыт, так взвинчен тишиною,
что скрипнет дверь иль книга упадет,
и — взрыв! и — все! и — кончено со мною!

and a piercing, electronic roller
swept its cold, green fire over my heart.

The dial was horrified! The hands leapt back!
The mercury started jumping up and down in fits!
Then came the deathbed crashing of the glass,
whose pieces sculpted blood from my fingertips.

"Watch out, good doctor; take another look!"
Unfazed, unflappable, he formally
announced: "Your pitiful, poor organism
has now begun to function normally."

That made me sad. I had been well aware
of my connection with this upper sphere.
Far too big to fit inside a mind,
its giant size floated in the air.

And schooled by my many-figured number of
ordeals, my nervous system, like a spring
breaking through a mattress, ripped my skin
and hissed and whistled at everything.

The enormous pulse that made my wrist so ugly
kept thundering, kept trying to get away.
Hell, let it go! As Petersburg choked on the Neva,
this is mine to swallow the wrong way.

Now at night my brain is sharp, expectant.
My ears, excited by the silence, are so keen
that the creaking of a door or a book's falling
is—bang!—explosion!—boom—the end of me!

Да, я не смела укротить зверей,
в меня вселенных, жрущих кровь из мяса.
При мне всегда стоял сквозняк дверей!
При мне всегда свеча, вдруг вспыхнув, гасла!

В моих зрачках, нависнув через край,
слезы светлела вечная громада.
Я — все собою портила! Я — рай
растлила б грозным неуютом ада.

Врач выписал мне должную латынь,
и с мудростью, цветущей в человеке,
как музыку по нотным запятым,
ее читала девушка в аптеке.

И вот теперь разнежен весь мой дом
целебным поцелуем валерьяны,
и медицина мятным языком
давно мои зализывает раны.

Сосед доволен, третий раз подряд
он поздравлял меня с выздоровленьем
через своих детей и, говорят,
хвалил меня пред домоуправленьем.

Я отдала визиты и долги,
ответила на письма. Я гуляю,
особо, с пользой делая круги.
Вина в шкафу держать не позволяю.

Вокруг меня — ни звука, ни души.
И стол мой умер и под пылью скрылся.
Уставили во тьму карандаши
тупые и неграмотные рыльца.
...

Indeed I never dared to tame the wild
animals in me that fed on blood from meat.
I always felt a draft from under doors!
I always saw the candle flare then die!

My pupils shone with gigantic pools of tears
that welled above the rims, ready to fall.
I spoiled it all myself! I would have corrupted
heaven with the dreadful wastes of hell.

The doctor wrote me out the proper Latin,
and—as some people are innately sage—
a young girl in the pharmacy then read it
as if reading music by black marks on a page.

Valerian's kiss-to-make-it-better touched
the tender feelings of my whole apartment house,
and for weeks the minty tongue of Medicine
has been licking my old wounds.

My neighbor's pleased. Three times he's had his children
report his joy at my recovery,
and he even has, I understand, extolled
me at a meeting of the Management Committee.

Visits I've returned, and debts paid back,
and even answered letters. I go walking myself,
intentionally, making useful circles.
I don't allow wine to be kept on the kitchen shelf.

There's not a sound around me, not a soul.
My table's dead; dust covers every part.
All my pencils aim their little blunt
illiterate snouts into the ignorant dark.

...

И, как у побежденного коня,
мой каждый шаг медлителен, стреножен.
Все хорошо! Но по ночам меня
опасное предчувствие тревожит.

Мой врач еще меня не уличил,
но зря ему я голову морочу,
ведь все, что он лелеял и лечил,
я разом обожгу иль обморожу.

Я, как улитка в костяном гробу,
спасаюсь слепотой и тишиною,
но, поболев, пощекотав во лбу,
рога антенн воспрянут надо мною.

О звездопад всех точек и тире,
зову тебя, осыпься! Пусть я сгину,
подрагивая в чистом серебре
русалочьих мурашек, жгущих спину!

Ударь в меня, как в бубен, не жалей,
озноб, я вся твоя! Не жить нам розно!
Я — балерина музыки твоей!
Щенок озябший твоего мороза!

Пока еще я не дрожу, о, нет,
сейчас о том не может быть и речи.
Но мой предусмотрительный сосед
уже со мною холоден при встрече.

As with a defeated racehorse, every step
I take is hobbled now and extra slow.
All's well, all's well! But every night I shake
with fear of things that I don't know.

My doctor hasn't yet declared me guilty,
but no point in pulling the wool over his eyes,
for everything that he has cured and cherished
I'll in an instant turn to fire or ice.

I, like a snail inside its bony coffin,
can save myself by being quiet and blind,
but falling sick, tingling in my forehead,
my antennae's horns will leap forth again.

O meteor shower of all dots and dashes,
come rain upon me! May I be lost to sight
while trembling from time to time in the pure silver
of a mermaid's gooseflesh burning up my spine!

Beat on me like a tambourine; don't spare me,
chills—I'm wholly yours! Apart, I'm lost!
I'm the ballerina of your music!
I'm the frozen puppy of your frost!

I haven't yet begun to shiver—not yet—
and even talking about it's against the rules;
but every time we meet my prudent neighbor
is already extremely cool.

ПРИМЕТЫ МАСТЕРСКОЙ

БОРИСУ МЕССЕРЕРУ

О гость грядущий, гость любезный!
Под этой крышей поднебесной,
которая одной лишь бездной
всевышней мглы превзойдена,
там, где четыре граммофона
взирают на тебя с амвона,
пируй и пей за время оно,
за граммофоны, за меня!

В какой немыслимой отлучке
я ныне пребываю, — лучше
не думать! Ломаной полушки
жаль на помин души моей,
коль не смогу твой пир обильный
потешить шуткой замогильной
и, как всеведущий Вергилий,
тебя не встречу у дверей.

Войди же в дом неимоверный,
где быт — в соседях со вселенной,
где вечности озноб мгновенный
был ведом людям и вещам,
и всплеск серебряных сердечек
о сквозняке пространств нездешних
гостей, когда-то здесь сидевших,
таинственно оповещал.

У ног, взошедших на Голгофу,
доверься моему глаголу
и, возведя себя на гору
поверх шестого этажа,
благослови любую малость,

FEATURES OF AN ARTIST'S STUDIO

FOR BORIS MESSERER

O future guest, guest most gentle!
Beneath this dear sublunar roof,
which only the unending bottom
of the All-mighty haze surmounts,
where from their pulpit four Victrolas
train their lordly eyes on you,
rejoice and sing to times a-passing,
to all Victrolas and me, too!

Better not to think about
the unimaginable distance
I'm at these days! Who'd spare a penny
for a candle for my soul
since I can't entertain your party
with a sepulchral joke or two
and, unlike Virgil the Omniscient,
am not at the door to welcome you?

Come into this fantastic house
where daily life is universal,
where things and people are familiar
with a sudden shudder of forever
and the splash of little silver hearts
mysteriously sends signals through
about the drafts from outer space
to guests who used to sit here, too.

At the feet that mounted Calvary,
trust in the words I say to you
and guide yourself upstairs slowly
past the sixth floor, singing praises
to every doodad and gilhickey,

почти предметов небывалость,
не смей, чтобы тебя боялась
шарманки детская душа.

Сверкнет ли в окнах луч закатный,
всплакнет ли ящик музыкальный
иль призрак севера печальный
вдруг вздыбит желтизну седин, —
пусть реет над юдолью скушной
дом, как заблудший шар воздушный,
чтоб ты, о гость мой простодушный,
чужбину неба посетил...

revere the fantasticality
of things, and don't let the barrel organ's
childlike spirit be scared of you.

Perhaps the sunset's in the window,
or the music box is shedding tears,
or for the Mournful Specter of the North
yellow stands on end among the gray—
long may the house, like a lost balloon,
flutter over Boredom Valley
so you, O artless guest of mine,
may reach this strange land in the sky.

Не уделяй мне много времени,
вопросов мне не задавай.
Глазами добрыми и верными
руки моей не задевай.

Не проходи весной по лужицам,
по следу следа моего.
Я знаю — снова не получится
из этой встречи ничего.

Ты думаешь, что я из гордости
хожу, с тобою не дружу?
Я не из гордости — из горести
так прямо голову держу.

[DON'T SPEND A LOT OF TIME ON ME]

Don't spend a lot of time on me;
no point in asking questions or
trying to pin my hands with your
    kind, faithful eyes.

In spring, no point in following me
through all the puddles. I know
that even if we meet again
    there's nothing more.

You think me proud to go everywhere
like this and not be friends with you?
Not pride but a heavy heart makes me
    hold my head high.

Прохожий, мальчик, что ты? Мимо
иди и не смотри мне вслед.
Мной тот любим, кем я любима!
К тому же знай: мне много лет.

Зрачков горячую угрюмость
вперять в меня повремени:
то смех любви, сверкнув, как юность,
позолотил черты мои.

Иду... февраль прохладой лечит
жар щек... и снегу намело
так много... и нескромно блещет
красой любви лицо мое.

[HEY, KID!]

Hey kid, passing by! What do you see?
Move on and don't dare be so bold.
I love my lover, who loves me.
And don't forget: I'm very old.

Wait a little before nailing me
with the sullen passion of your dark eyes:
flashing by like youth, love's laughter
has stained my looks with golden dyes.

So, I go . . . The February
cold draws the fever from my face . . .
The snow is high . . . Immodestly
I radiate love's inner grace.

ВОЗВРАЩЕНИЕ В ТАРУСУ

Пред Окой преклоненность земли,
и к Тарусе томительный подступ.
Медлил в этой глубокой пыли
стольких странников горестный посох.

Нынче май, и растет желтизна
из открытой земли и расщелин.
Грустным знаньем душа стеснена:
этот миг бытия совершенен.

К церкви беховской ластится глаз.
Раз еще оглянусь — и довольно.
Я б сказала, что жизнь удалась,
все сбылось и нисколько не больно.

Просьбы нет у пресыщенных уст
к благолепью цветущей равнины.
О, как сир этот рай и как пуст,
если правда, что нет в нем Марины.

RETURN TO TARUSA

The land kneels down before the Oka;
the Tarusa road is a weary way.
The mournful staffs of hundreds of pilgrims
moved slow in the dust in olden days.

Now it's May, and a world of yellow
bursts from turned-over earth and clefts.
The soul is constrained by its sad knowing:
this moment of being is complete.

My eye is drawn to Bekhovo Church.
Then back I look— Good enough; it'll do.
I'd say that life's not a bad success—
not at all—and everything came true.

Sated lips have no favor to ask
of the grandeur of the flowering plain.
O how lonely this heaven is,
how empty, if Marina's gone.

Кто знает — вечность или миг
мне предстоит бродить по свету.
За этот миг иль вечность эту
равно благодарю я мир.

Что б ни случилось, не кляну,
а лишь благословляю легкость:
твоей печали мимолетность,
моей кончины тишину.

[WHO KNOWS]

Who knows how long I have to wander
the earth—forever or a day.
For a moment or for ever—
I thank the world for either way.

Whatever happens I won't start swearing
but bless life's easy ebb and flow:
the fleeting nature of your grieving
and the silence of my letting go.

ЛАДЫЖИНО

Я этих мест не видела давно.
Душа во сне глядит в чужие краи
на тех, моих, кого люблю, кого
у этих мест и у меня — украли.

Душе во сне в чужую даль глядеть
досуга нет — но и вчера глядела.
Я думала, когда проснулась здесь:
душе не внове будет взмыв из тела.

Так вот на что я променяла вас,
друзья души, обобранной разбоем.
К вам солнце шло. Мой день вчерашний гас.
Вы — за Окой, вон там, за тёмным бором.

И ваши слёзы видели в ночи
меня в Тарусе, что одно и то же.
Нашли меня и долго прочь не шли.
Чем сон нежней, тем пробужденье строже.

Вот новый день, который вам пошлю —
оповестить о сердца разрываньи,
когда иду по снегу и по льду
сквозь бор и бездну между мной и вами.

Так я вхожу в Ладыжино. Просты
черты красы и бедствия родного.
О, тётя Маня, смилуйся, прости
меня за всё, за слово и не-слово.

Прогорк твой лик, твой малый дом убог.
Моих друзей и у тебя отняли.

LADYZHINO

I had not been back for many years.
I often dreamed of foreign lands and the faces
of people I once loved, the people who
were taken from me and from their native place.

There has never been the time to dream beyond
the horizon—but then yesterday I did.
On waking here, I thought: in no way strange
that soul should fly from body like a bird.

I have bartered you for this, friends
of a plundered heart picked clean as bone.
The sun joined you (my yesterday went out)
across the Oka in a forest dark like stone.

Night after night your tears saw me in Tarusa,
which for us both was the same as the real thing.
They found me there and did not go away:
the sweeter the dream, the harsher the awakening.

Now here is a new dawn, a day I send
to keep you up-to-date on how my heart breaks
every time I cross the snow and ice
of the chasm and dark forest that lie between us.

Look: I am walking into Ladyzhino.
The charms and catastrophes of home are plain.
O Aunty Manya, take pity on me, forgive
me everything I said and did not say.

You look embittered; your house is but a hovel;
my friends were taken from you, too, one night.

Всё слышу: «Не печалься, голубок».
Да мочи в сердце меньше, чем печали.

Окно во снег, икона, стол, скамья.
Ад глаз моих за рукавом я прячу.
«Ах, ангел мой, желанная моя,
не плачь, не сетуй».
Сетую и плачу.

And still you say, "Don't be so miserable."
Oh, a heart contains more misery than might.

Snow outside. An ikon, bench and table—
I hide my inside hell behind my sleeve.
"Ah, angel, welcome one, my prodigal,
no weeping, no laments."
I lament and weep.

ДВА ГЕПАРДА

Этот ад, этот сад, этот зоо —
там, где лебеди и зоосад,
на прицеле всеобщего взора
два гепарда, обнявшись, лежат.

Шерстью в шерсть, плотью в плоть проникая,
сердцем втиснувшись в сердце — века
два гепарда лежат. О, какая,
два гепарда, какая тоска!

Смотрит глаз в золотой, безвоздушный,
равный глаз безысходной любви.
На потеху толпе простодушной
обняись и лежат, как легли.

Прихожу ли я к ним, ухожу ли —
не слабее с той давней поры
их объятье густое, как джунгли,
и сплошное, как камень горы.

Обнялись — остальное неправда,
ни утрат, ни оград, ни преград.
Только так, только так, два гепарда,
я-то знаю, гепард и гепард.

TWO CHEETAHS

Here in this hell, this garden, this zoo
 this zoological garden with swans,
as the target everyone is looking at
 two cheetahs lie in each other's arms.

Fur next to fur, flesh deep in flesh,
 hearts pressed tight together, two
cheetahs have been lying here
 forever—what longing!—with nothing to do.

Eye looks at golden, airless eye
 in endless love on an equal plane.
To amuse the silly visitors
 they embrace and lie down as they have lain.

Whether I approach or turn away,
 their embrace, as firm as a granite slope
and thick like a jungle's undergrowth,
 remains as strong as long ago.

The fact: they embraced. The fence and their losses
 and everything else is really not true.
Two cheetahs are here for no reason I know—
 Cheetah One and Cheetah Two.

ШУМ ТИШИНЫ

Преодолима с Паршином разлука
мечтой ума и соучастьем ног.
Для ловли необщительного звука
искомого — я там держу силок.

Мне следовало в комнате остаться —
и в ней есть для добычи западня.
Но рознь была занятием пространства,
и мысль об этом увлекла меня.

Я шла туда, где разворот простора
наивелик. И вот он был каков:
замкнув меня, как сжатие острога,
сцепились интересы сквозняков.

Заокский воин поднял меч весенний.
Ответный норд призвал на помощь ост.
Вдобавок задувало из вселенной.
(Ужасней прочих этот ветер звезд.)

Не пропадать же в схватке исполинов!
Я — из людей, и отпустите прочь.
Но мелкий сброд незримых, неповинных
в делах ее — не занимает ночь.

С избытком мне хватало недознанья.
Я просто шла, чтобы услышать звук,
я не бросалась в прорубь мирозданья,
да зданье ли — весь этот бред вокруг?

Ни шевельнуться, ни дохнуть — нет мочи.
Кто рядом был? Чьи мне слова слышны?

THE NOISE OF SILENCE

Parting from Parshino can be overcome
by mental fancy and by feet taking part.
To catch the solitary sound of the x
I long for, I keep a noose of wire there.

I was supposed to stay on in my room—
it has a trap for catching lots of game—
but space was showing its hostility,
and the thought of that carried me away.

I walked to where the growth of spaciousness
is greatest. And this is how I now report it:
having locked me in, as if squeezing me in jail,
the crosswinds started struggling with each other.

The Trans-Oka warrior raised his vernal sword;
the North Wind in reply called up the East;
then, too, it started blowing from outer space.
(This starry wind is by far the worst.)

To perish in the giants' battle—no!
I am a person; let me go on my way!
But small fry, unseen and uninvolved
in what she does, do not interest Night.

There was so much I could not fathom it.
I kept on going in order to hear a sound,
did not dive down the hole through structured space—
if structured it is, this madness all around.

I had no more strength to move or even breathe.
Who was beside me? Whose words did I now hear?

— Шум тишины — вот содержанье ночи...
Шум тишины... — и вновь: шум тишины...

И только-то? За этим ли трофеем
я шла в разлад и разнобой весны,
в разъятый ад, проведанный Орфеем?
Как нежно он сказал: шум тишины...

Шум тишины стоял в открытом поле.
На воздух — воздух шел, и тьма на тьму.
Четыре сильных кругосветных воли
делили ночь по праву своему.

Я в дом вернулась. Ахнули соседи:
— Где были вы? Что там, где были вы?
— Шум тишины главенствует на свете.
Близ Паршина была. Там спать легли.

Бессмыслица, нескладица, мне — долго
любить тебя. Но веки тяжелы.
Шум тишины... сон подступает... только
шум тишины... шум только тишины...

The noise of silence was what the night contained . . .
The noise of silence . . . The noise of silence again . . .

And only it? Was that the prize for which
I took up arms in combat with the spring?
went through the hell that Orpheus once knew?
How tenderly he said, "The noise of silence . . ."

The noise of silence stood in an open field.
Air moved over air; dark, over darkness.
According to their rights, four monstrous earth-
embracing wills divided up the night.

I got back home. My neighbors were upset:
"Where were you?" "Tell us!" "Come on, where?" "Go ahead!"
"The noise of silence has commandeered the world.
I was near Parshino." Then we went to bed.

Absurdity and nonsense, I mean to love
you deeply very long, but my eyes are heavy.
The noise of silence . . . I feel sleep coming . . . just
the noise of silence . . . the noise of silence only . . .

ЗВУК УКАЗУЮЩИЙ

Звук указующий, десятый день
я жду тебя на Паршинской дороге.
И снова жду под полною луной.
Звук указующий, ты где-то здесь.
Пади в отверстой раны плодородье.
Зачем таишься и следишь за мной?

Звук указующий, пусть велика
моя вина, но велика и мука.
И чей, как мой, тобою слух любим?
Меня прощает полная луна.
Но нет мне указующего звука.
Нет звука мне. Зачем он прежде был?

Ни с кем моей луной не поделюсь,
да и она другого не полюбит.
Жизнь замечает вдруг, что — пред-мертва.
Звук указующий, я предаюсь
игре с твоим отсутствием подлунным.
Звук указующий, прости меня.

SOUND POINTING THE WAY

Sound pointing the way, directional sound,
I've been waiting for you on the Parshino road
for ten days; the moon's again full.
Sound pointing the way, you're somewhere around.
Land on the flesh of my open wound.
Why do you hide but keep following me?

Sound pointing the way, my guilt may be great,
but great is my suffering, too. Indeed, do you
like anyone's hearing more than mine?
The full moon forgives me my trespasses.
But there's no sound pointing the way.
I hear no sound. Why did I before?

I won't share my moon with anyone;
indeed, there's no one else that it would love.
Life suddenly smells death coming.
Sound pointing the way, I'm caught up in a game
played with your absence in the moonlight.
Sound pointing the way, forgive me.

ЕЛКА В БОЛЬНИЧНОМ КОРИДОРЕ

В коридоре больничном поставили елку. Она
и сама смущена, что попала в обитель страданий.
В край окна моего ленинградская входит луна
и недолго стоит: много окон и много стояний.

К той старухе, что бойко бедует на свете одна,
переходит луна, и доносится шорох стараний
утаить от соседок, от злого непрочного сна
нарушенье порядка, оплошность запретных рыданий.

Всем больным стало хуже. Но все же — канун Рождества.
Завтра кто-то дождется известий, гостинцев, свиданий.
Жизнь со смертью — в соседях. Каталка всегда не пуста —
лифт в ночи отскрипит равномерность ее упаданий.

Вечно радуйся, Дева! Младенца ты в ночь принесла.
Оснований других не оставлено для упований,
но они так важны, так огромны, так несть им числа,
что прощен и утешен безвестный затворник подвальный.

Даже здесь, в коридоре, где елка — причина для слез
(не хотели ее, да сестра заносить повелела),
сердце бьется и слушает, и — раздалось, донеслось:
— Эй, очнитесь! Взгляните — восходит Звезда Вифлеема.

Достоверно одно: воздыханье коровы в хлеву,
поспешанье волхвов, и неопытной матери локоть,
упасавший младенца с отметиной чудной во лбу.
Остальное — лишь вздор, затянувшейся лжи мимолетность.
...

THE HOSPITAL
CHRISTMAS TREE

They have set a Christmas tree up in a hospital ward.
It clearly feels out of place in a cloister of suffering.
The moon over Leningrad comes to my window ledge
but does not stay long—many windows, much waiting.

The moon moves on to a spry, independent old woman;
outside you can hear the susurrous sound of her trying
to hide from her neighbors and from her own shallow sleep
her breaking the norm—the blunder of illegal crying.

All the patients are worse; still, it is Christmas Eve.
Tomorrow some will get news; some, gifts; some, calls.
Life and death remain neighbors: the stretcher is always
   loaded;
through the long night the elevator squeaks as it falls.

Rejoice eternally, Virgin! You bore The Child at night.
There is no other reason for hope, but that matters so much,
is so huge, so eternally endless, that it
consoles the unknown, underground anchorite.

Even here in the ward where the tree makes some people cry
(did not want it; a nurse, in fact, ordered it brought)
the listening heart beats, and you hear people say,
"Hey, look! The Star of Bethlehem's in the sky!"

The only sure facts are the cattle's lament in the shed,
the Wise Men's haste, the inexperienced mother's elbow
marking The Child with a miraculous spot on His brow.
All the rest is absurd, an age-old but fugitive lie.

...

Этой плоти больной, извреженной трудом и войной,
что нужней и отрадней столь просто описанной сцены?
Но — корят то вином, то другою какою виной
и питают умы рыбьей костью обглоданной схемы.

Я смотрела, как день занимался в десятом часу:
каплей был и блестел, как бессмысленный черный фонарик, —
там, в окне и вовне. Но прислышалось общему сну:
в колокольчик на елке названивал крошка звонарик.

Занимавшийся день был так слаб, неумел, неказист.
Цвет — был меньше чем розовый: родом из робких, нерезких.
Так на девичьей шее умеет мерцать аметист.
Все потупились, глянув на кроткий и жалобный крестик.

А как стали вставать, с неохотой глаза открывать, —
вдоль метели пронесся трамвай, изнутри золотистый.
Все столпились у окон, как дети: — Вот это трамвай!
Словно окунь, ушедший с крючка: весь пятнистый, огнистый.

Сели завтракать, спорили, вскоре устали, легли.
Из окна вид таков, что невидимости Ленинграда
или невидали мне достанет для слез и любви.
— Вам не надо ль чего-нибудь? — Нет, ничего нам не надо.

Мне пеняли давно, что мои сочиненья пусты.
Сочинитель пустот, в коридоре смотрю на сограждан.
Матерь божия! Смилуйся! Сына о том же проси.
В день рожденья его дай молиться и плакать о каждом!

What matters more or brings more joy to sick flesh
wasted by work and by war than so simple a scene?
But they reproach you for drinking or some other fault
and stuff your brain with the bones of a system picked clean.

I watched the day begin breaking some time past nine;
it was a drop, a black light shining absurdly
onto the window. People dreamt that they heard
a little toy bell-ringer ringing the bell on the tree.

The day as it dawned was weak, not much of a sight.
The light was paler than pink, pastel, not harsh,
the way an amethyst shimmers on a young girl's neck.
All looked down, once they had seen the sad, humble cross.

And when they arose, reluctantly opening their eyes,
a trolley flew by through the snowstorm, gold trim inside it.
They crowded the window like children: "Hey, look at that car!
Like a perch that's gotten away, all speckled with fire!"

They sat down to breakfast; they argued, got tired, lay down.
The view from the window was such that Leningrad's secrets
and splendors brought tears to my eyes, filled me with love.
"Isn't there something you want?" "No, there's nothing."

I have long been accused of making up frivolous things.
Frivolity maker, I look at those here around me:
O Mother of God, have mercy! And beg your Son, too.
On the day of His birth, pray and weep for us each.

С А Д/В С А Д Н И К

За этот ад,
за этот бред,
пошли мне сад
на старость лет.

Марина Цветаева

Сад-всадник летит по отвесному склону.
Какое сверканье и буря какая!
В плаще его черном лицо мое скрою,
к защите его старшинства приникая.

Я помню, я знаю, что дело нечисто.
Вовек не бывало столь позднего часа,
в котором сквозь бурю он скачет и мчится,
в котором сквозь бурю один уже мчался.

Но что происходит? Кто мчится, кто скачет?
Где конь отыскался для всадника сада?
И нет никого, но приходится с каждым
о том толковать, чего знать им не надо.

Сад-всадник свои покидает угодья
и гриву коня в него ветер бросает.
Одною рукою он держит поводья,
другою мой страх на груди упасает.

О сад-охранитель! Невиданно львиный
чей хвост так разгневан? Чья блещет корона?
— Не бойся! То — длинный туман над равниной,
то — желтый заглавный огонь Ориона.

Но слышу я голос насмешки всевластной:
— Презренный младенец за пазухой отчей!

THE GARDEN / THE GUARDSMAN

For the hell we live in,
for this mad rage,
send me a garden
for my old age.
 —Marina Tsvetaeva

The garden / the guardsman flies down the steep slope.
What shimmering light! What a hurricane!
I hide my face in his jet-black cape,
drawing close to his older self to keep safe.

I remember, I know, the whole thing is suspicious.
There never has been an hour so late
when he was galloping through a wild storm,
when braving a storm he had already faced.

What then is happening? Who rushes? Who gallops?
Where did the garden pick up a steed?
Really, there's no one—well, everyone then
must listen to things he never should hear.

The garden / the guardsman quits his good farmland,
and the wind whips the horse's mane in his face.
He holds the reins in one hand; with the other
he assuages the fear that beats in my breast.

O garden / my guardian! Whose unexpectedly
leonine tail is so angry? Whose crown so shines?
"Relax! That's only a fog on the plain,
and the yellow light that haloes Orion."

But I hear a voice of omnipotent mockery:
"Contemptible infant in its father's bosom!

Короткая гибель под царскою лаской —
навечнее пагубы денной и нощной.

О всадник родитель, дай тьмы и теплыни!
Вернемся в отчизну обрыва-отшиба!
С хвостом и в короне смеется: — Толпы ли,
твои ли то речи, избранник-ошибка?

Другим не бывает столь позднего часа.
Он впору тебе. Уж не будет так поздно.
Гнушаюсь тобою! Со мной не прощайся!
Сад-всадник мне шепчет: — Не слушай, не бойся.

Живую меня он приносит в обитель
на тихой вершине отвесного склона.
О сад мой, заботливый мой погубитель!
Зачем от Царя мы бежали Лесного?

Сад делает вид, что он — сад, а не всадник,
что слово Лесного Царя отвратимо.
И нет никого, но склоняюсь пред всяким:
все было дано, а судьбы не хватило.

Сад дважды играет с обрывом родимым:
с откоса в Оку, как пристало изгою,
летит он ныряльщиком необратимым
и увальнем вымокшим тащится в гору.

Мы оба притворщики. Полночью черной,
в завременьи позднем, сад-всадник несется.
Ребенок, Лесному Царю обреченный,
да не убоится, да не упасется.

Quick death that comes from a kind, royal hand
is more everlasting than day-and-night ruin."

O guardsman my father, grant darkness, warm weather!
Let's return to the country where all lived apart!
With his tail and his crown he laughs back: "Are there crowds?
Or are you doing the talking, Chosen Mistake?

"No others are granted an hour so late.
It's in good time for you. It won't be so late any longer.
You I abhor! Don't consider saying good-bye!"
The garden / my guardsman advises: "Don't listen, relax."

He then guides the real, living me to a shelter
on the silent peak of the steep, steep slope.
O my garden, my kind, conscientious destroyer!
Why did we flee from the Tsar of the Woods?

The garden pretends it's a garden, no guardsman,
that the word of the Tsar can still be averted.
Although really there's no one, I bow low to any:
all had been given, but Fate ran out.

The garden redoubles the cut it was born with:
from the social misfit of its Oka-bound slope
it flies like an irreversible diver
and limps, like a soaking wet bumpkin, uphill.

We're con artists both. In the dead of the night,
in time beyond time, the garden / the guardsman sails on.
May the infant doomed to the Tsar of the Woods
neither ever know fear nor ever be saved.

Чудовищный и призрачный курорт —
услада для заезжих чужестранцев.
Их привечает пристальный урод
(знать, больше нет благообразных старцев),
и так порочен этот вождь ворот,
что страшно за рассеянных скитальцев.
Простят ли мне Кирилл и Ферапонт,
что числилась я в списке постояльцев?

Я — невиновна. Произволен блат:
стихолюбивы дивы «Интуриста».
Одни лишь финны, гости финских блат,
не ощущают никакого риска,
когда красотка поднимает взгляд,
в котором хлад стоит и ад творится.
Но я не вхожа в этот хладный ад:
всегда моя потуплена зеница.

Вид из окна: сосна и «мерседес».
Пир под сосной мои пресытил уши.
Официант, рожденный для злодейств,
погрязнуть должен в мелочи и в чуши.

Отечество, ты приютилось здесь
подобострастно и как будто вчуже.
Но разнобой моих ночных сердец
всегда тебя подозревает в чуде.

Ни разу я не выходила прочь
из комнаты. И предается думе
прислуга (вся в накрапе зримых порч):
от бедности моей или от дури?
...

Phantasmagoric monster, the health resort
titillates the foreign tourists' tastes.
A hideous freak stares them in and out
(no noble elders living now, I guess),
a gatekeeper so filled with moral rot
that you worry over all the drifting homeless.
Will Cyril and Ferapont forgive me that
my name is on the register of guests?

It's not my fault. Influence is capricious:
Intourist's prima donnas love poetry.
Only the Finns, who bribe to get their wishes,
never have a sense of risqué or risky
when some good-looking girl gives them a frigid
glance prefiguring the hell to be.
That icy hell has nothing to do with me:
I keep my eyes always looking down.

The view from the window: Pine Tree with Mercedes.
The party under the pine has burst my ears.
The waiter, born for great and wicked deeds,
must soil his hands with details and stupidities.

My fatherland, sheltered here, you are,
it seems, too vicarious and much too servile,
but the different tempos of my midnight hearts
always hold you suspect of some marvel.

I have not left my room a single time.
Under the drizzly spell of the evil eye
the chambermaid has begun to think
it must be silliness—or poverty.

...

Пейзаж усилен тем, что вдвинут «порш»
в невидимые мне залив и дюны.
И, кроме мысли, никаких нет почт,
чтоб грусть моя достигла тети Дюни.

Чтоб городок Кириллов позабыть,
отправлюсь-ка проведать жизнь иную.
Дежурной взгляд незряч, но остро-быстр.
О, я в снэк-бар всего лишь, не в пивную.

Ликуют финны. Рада я за них.
Как славно пьют, как весело одеты.
Пускай себе! Ведь это — их залив.
А я — подкидыш, сдуру взятый в дети.

С улыбкой собеседники следят:
смотри, коль слово лишнее проронишь.
Но не сидеть же при гостях в слезах?
Так осмелел, что пьет коньяк приемыш.

Финн вопросил: "Where are you from, madame?"
Приятно поболтать с негоциантом.
— Оттеда я, где черт нас догадал
произрасти с умом да и с талантом.

Он поражен: с талантом и умом?
И этих свойств моя не ценит фирма?
Не перейти ль мне в их торговый дом?
— Спасибо, нет, — благодарю я финна.

Мне повезло: никто не внял словам
того, чья слава множится и крепнет:
ни финн, ни бармен — гордый внук славян,
ну а тунгусов не пускают в кемпинг.
...

The view is aggravated by a Porsche parked
before the Gulf and dunes I have not seen.
Except for thoughts, I have no postal means
for sending Aunty Dunya my sad feelings.

To take Kirillov Village off my mind
I think I'll set out for another life.
The concierge's glance is dull but very quick.
Oh, I'm not going for a drink but for a snack.

The Finns exult. I'm very glad for them.
How wonderfully they drink; how brightly dress—
Why shouldn't they? After all, the Gulf is theirs.
And I'm but a foundling adopted out of foolishness.

The people talking to me softly smile:
careful lest you breathe a needless word.
Can one sit crying, though, in front of guests?
The foster child boldly had a brandy.

A Finn asked me: "Where are you from, Madame?"
I liked talking to a businessman.
"I come from where clever Satan taught
us all to grow up talented and smart."

That astounds him. Talented and smart?
"And my company doesn't take those qualities in?"
Would I like to transfer to his firm?
"Thanks, but no thanks," I thank the Finn.

I came out lucky. No one paid attention
to the words of one whose glory grows and strengthens—
not the Finn, not the barman (proud Slavic grandson);
besides, Tunguses can't get into campgrounds.
...

Спасибо, нет, мне хорошо лишь здесь,
где зарасту бессмертной лебедою.
Кириллов же и ближний Белозерск
сокроются под вечною водою.

Что ж, тете Дюне — девяностый год, —
финн речь заводит об архитектуре, —
а правнуков ее большой народ
мечтает лишь о финском гарнитуре.

Тут я смеюсь. Мой собеседник рад.
Он говорит, что поставляет мебель
в столь знаменитый близлежащий град,
где прежде он за недосугом не был.

Когда б не он — кто бы наладил связь
бессвязных дум? Уж если жить в мотеле
причудливом — то лучше жить смеясь,
не то рехнуться можно в самом деле.

В снэк-баре — смех, толкучка, красота,
и я любуюсь финкой молодою:
уж так свежа (хоть несколько толста).
Я выхожу, иду к чужому дому,
и молвят Ферапонтовы уста
над бывшей и грядущею юдолью:
«Земля была безвидна и пуста,
и Божий дух носился над водою».

Thanks, but no thanks. Here is where I'm fine,
where the immortal goosefoot heals me over.
Kirillov Village and nearby Belozersk
will disappear beneath eternal waters.

And so—Aunty Dunya is eighty-nine—
the Finn begins a speech on architecture—
but her grandchildren that make up one vast people
dream only of a Finnish bedroom suite.

That makes me laugh. The man I'm talking to
is glad, for he's a furniture supplier
to a very famous city close to me
which formerly he had no time to see.

If not for him, wouldn't somebody
have tied such untied minds together? The art
of living in a fantastical motel
means laughing lest you really fall apart.

There's laughter in the snack bar, crowds and beauty—
I can't help admiring a Finnish woman, young
and oh so fresh (although a little heavy).
And then I leave, and go to someone's house,
and the lips of Ferapont begin to speak
above the valley of the past and future:
The earth was lacking shape and form, and void,
and the Holy Spirit swept across the waters.

ДРУГОЕ

Что сделалось? Зачем я не могу,
уж целый год не знаю, не умею
слагать стихи и только немоту
тяжелую в моих губах имею?

Вы скажете — но вот уже строфа,
четыре строчки в ней, она готова.
Я не о том. Во мне уже стара
привычка ставить слово после слова.

Порядок этот ведает рука.
Я не о том. Как это прежде было?
Когда происходило — не строка —
другое что-то. Только что? — Забыла.

Да, то, другое, разве знало страх,
когда шалило голосом так смело,
само, как смех, смеялось на устах
и плакало, как плач, если хотело?

SOMETHING ELSE

"What's happened? For the past year I haven't been able
to write a poem—no longer seem to know how—
have lost the knack—possess nothing tangible
but a heavy dumbness that fills my mouth."

You'll say, "But look, now you have a stanza.
Four lines, a quatrain, part of a whole prepared—"
"That's not what I'm talking about. It's second nature
for me to slap lines together, word after word.

"The hand's the one in charge of such arrangements.
No, that's not what I'm talking about at all.
I meant, before, when it wasn't just verse that happened
but something else. What was it? I can't recall.

"I wonder if it felt a sense of fear
back when it had my voice boldly misbehaving
and it laughed like laughter on my open lips
and wept like weeping anytime it wanted?"

СТРОКА

...Дорога не скажу куда...

Анна Ахматова

Пластинки глупенькое чудо,
проигрыватель — вздор какой,
и слышно, как невесть откуда,
из недр стесненных, из-под спуда
корней, сопревших трав и хвой,
где закипает перегной,
вздымая пар до небосвода,
нет, глубже мыслимых глубин,
из пекла, где пекут рубин
и начинается природа, —
исторгнут, близится, и вот
донесся бас земли и вод,
которым молвлено протяжно,
как будто вовсе без труда,
так легкомысленно, так важно:
«...Дорога не скажу куда...»
Меж нами так не говорят,
нет у людей такого знанья,
ни вымыслом, ни наугад
тому не подыскать названья,
что мы, в невежестве своем,
строкой бессмертной назовем.

THE LINE

"... *A road I won't say leading where ...*"
—*Anna Akhmatova*

What silly marvels records are,
and record players—plastic boodle,
with lots of sound God knows from where,
from unknown depths beneath a bushel
of roots and rotted grass and needles
where compost's steaming like a kettle,
rising to the vault of heaven—
nay, deeper than mind thinks or heart aches,
from the fiery hell where the ruby's baked
and nature's dough is punched and leavened—
ostracized but drawing near,
it's earth and water's bass we hear
speaking to us languidly
but as easily as breathing air,
so offhandedly, so grandly:
"... A road I won't say leading where ..."
Between us no one talks like that;
no one has that kind of knowledge;
no random quest, no fancy flight
will help one get the title right
of what from ignorance we define
    as an immortal line.

ДЕНЬ-РАФАЭЛЬ

Пришелец День, не стой на розовом холме!
Не дай, чтобы заря твоим чертам грубила.
Зачем ты снизошел к оврагам и ко мне?
Я узнаю тебя. Ты родом из Урбино.

День-Божество, ступай в Италию свою.
У нас еще зима. У нас народ балует.
Завистник и горбун, я на тебя смотрю
и край твоих одежд мой тайный гнев целует.

Ах, мало оспы щек и гнилости в груди,
еще и кисть глупа и краски непослушны.
День-Совершенство, сгинь! Прочь от греха уйди!
Здесь за корсаж ножи всегда кладут пастушки.

Но ласково глядел Богоподобный День.
И брату брат сказал: «Брат досточтимый, здравствуй!»
Престольный праздник трех окрестных деревень
впервые за века не завершился дракой.

Неузнанным ушел День-Свет, День-Рафаэль.
Но мёртвый дуб расцвел средь ровныя долины.
И благостный закат над нами розовел.
И странники всю ночь крестились на руины.

RAPHAEL'S DAY

Newcomer Day, don't stop on the rosy hill!
Don't let the dawn treat your features rudely.
Why deign come down to the gullies and to me?
I recognize you. You're straight from Urbino.

Divinity Day, go back to your Italy.
It's winter here. People are screwing around.
A hunchback filled with envy, I look at you
and my hidden rage kisses the hem of your gown.

On top of pock-marked cheeks and chest rotting in,
my brush is silly and the colors won't behave.
Perfection Day, get out! Away from sin!
Here shepherdesses' vests conceal sharp knives.

But the God-like Day kept watching tenderly,
and brother said to brother, "Good brother, hello!"
For the time in years, the Saint's Day festival
Of three neighboring villages didn't end in blows.

Unknown, it left—Raphael's Day, Day of Light—
but a dead oak in the open valley blossomed;
above us the blessed sun turned rose; all night
pilgrims made the sign of the cross among the ruins.

В том времени, где и злодей —
лишь заурядный житель улиц,
как грозно хрупок иудей,
в ком Русь и музыка очнулись.

Вступленье: ломкий силуэт,
повинный в грациозном форсе.
Начало века. Младость лет.
Сырое лето в Гельсингфорсе.

Та — бог иль барышня? Мольба —
чрез сотни вёрст любви нечёткой.
Любуется! И гений лба
застенчиво завешен чёлкой.

Но век желает пировать!
Измученный, он ждёт предлога —
и Петербургу Петроград
оставит лишь предсмертье Блока.

Знал и сказал, что будет знак
и век падёт ему на плечи.
Что может он? Он нищ и наг
пред чудом им свершённой речи.

Ему — особенный почёт,
двоякое злорадство неба,
певец, снабжённый кляпом в рот,
и лакомка, лишённый хлеба.

Гортань, затеявшая речь
неслыханную, — так открыта.

[IN MEMORY OF O. MANDELSHTAM]

Back in the days when any villain would do—
   was merely the man in the street—
how threateningly fragile the faithful Jew
   who sang of the glory of Rus'.

The opening scene: a frail silhouette
   controlled by a graceful mummer;
the century begun; he, young yet;
   in Helsingfors, a raw summer.

Then She—god or maid? And he on his knees
   across miles of unspoken love.
She loves to look! His high brow, she sees,
   is modestly covered up.

But the anxious age wants to celebrate!
   It's looking for an excuse
while Petrograd city gives Petersburg back
   the dying Blok's last truths.

He knew and said there would be a sign
   that the age would fall on his shoulders.
What else could he do? He stood dumb but condign
   before the miraculous language.

Special honors to him in his role as poet,
   and double god's wicked delight
at the singer whose song was plugged in his throat
   and the lover of sweets wanting bread.

So open the throat that let out the voice
   creating original speech!

Довольно, чтоб её пресечь
и меньшего усердья быта.

Из мемуаров: «Мандельштам
любил пирожные». Я рада
узнать об этом. Но дышать —
не хочется, да и не надо.

Так значит, пребывать творцом,
за спину заломивши руки,
и безымянным мертвецом,
всё ж недостаточно для муки?

И в смерти надо знать беду
той, не утихшей ни однажды,
беспечной, выжившей в аду,
неутолимой детской жажды?

В моём кошмаре, в том раю,
где жив он, где его я прячу,
он сыт! И я его кормлю
огромной сладостью! И плачу!

All they did was cut it across
 for life to seem out of reach.

The memoirs declare: "Poet Mandelshtam
 went wild over pastry." I'm glad
to know that. But, whatever I am,
 why breathe? Why, even, go mad?

Does it mean that to keep on being a poet,
 hands wrung behind your back,
then a corpse with a name (but no one knows it),
 you need torture to fill a lack?

And, dead, you have to feel the loss
 of that endless, childlike hope
that took you mindlessly across
 hell toward your unreachable goal?

In one of my nightmares, where he hides forever
 in a heaven I hold dear,
he's satisfied. I feed him sweetness—
 lots of sweetness—and shed tears.

СМЕРТЬ СОВЫ

Кривая Нинка: нет зубов, нет глаза.
При этом — зла. При этом... Боже мой,
кем и за что наведена проказа
на этот лик, на этот край глухой?

С получки загуляют Нинка с братом —
подробности я удержу в уме.
Брат Нинку бьет. Он не рожден горбатым:
отец был строг, век вековал в тюрьме.

Теперь он, слышно, старичок степенный —
да не пускают дети на порог.
И то сказать: наш километр — сто первый.
Злодеи мы. Нас не жалеет Бог.

Вот не с получки было. В сени к Нинке
сова внеслась. Ты не коси, а вдарь!
Ведром ее! Ей — смерть, а нам — поминки.
На чучело художник купит тварь.

И он купил. Я относила книгу
художнику и у его дверей
посторонилась, пропуская Нинку,
и, как всегда, потупилась при ней.

Не потому, что уродились розно, —
наоборот, у нас судьба одна.
Мне в жалостных чертах её уродства
видна моя погибель и вина.

Вошла. Безумье вспомнило: когда-то
мне этих глаз являлась нагота.

AN OWL'S DEATH

Crooked little one-eyed toothless Nina:
malicious, too. Moreover—oh, my god,
why would any face be so disfigured,
like this far-off, godforsaken land?

On payday, Nina and her brother always
tie one on. I'll spare you the details.
The brother beats her up. How come he's hunchbacked?
Their cruel father spent half his life in jail,

but has become, I hear, a staid old man,
though the children still won't let him in the house.
And right they are: out here's the end of the line;
we're villains all; God feels no pity for us.

One day that wasn't payday an owl by mistake
got in the entry hall. "Don't stand there squinting!
Hit it! It kicks the bucket—we have a wake!
The painter'll buy the thing to have it mounted."

Indeed, he did. When I was taking back
a book I borrowed, I met Nina in the doorway
and stepped aside to let her through as always
looking down whenever we two passed

not because we started life so differently—
on the contrary, our fortunes are the same—
but in the pitiful lines of her deformity
I see my own destruction and my shame.

I went in. That folly reminded me: I had seen
the nakedness of those eyes some time ago.

В два нежных, в два безвыходных агата
смерть Божества смотрела — но куда?

Умеет так, без направленья взгляда,
звезда смотреть, иль то, что ей сродни,
то, старшее, чему уже не надо
гадать: в чем смысл? — отверстых тайн среди.

Какой ценою ни искупим — вряд ли
простит нас Тот, кто нарядил сову
в дрожь карих радуг, в позолоту ряби,
в беспомощную белизну свою.

Очнулась я. Чтобы столиц приветы
достигли нас, транзистор поднял крик.
Зловещих лиц пригожие портреты
повсюду улыбались вкось и вкривь.

Успела я сказать пред расставаньем
художнику: — Прощайте, милый мэтр.
Но как вы здесь? Вам, с вашим рисованьем, —
поблажка наш сто первый километр.

Взамен зари — незнаемого цвета
знак розовый помедлил и погас,
словно вопрос, который ждал ответа,
но не дождался и покинул нас.

Жива ль звезда, я думала, что длится
передо мною и вокруг меня?
Или она, как доблестная птица,
умеет быть прекрасна и мертва?

Смерть: сени, двух уродов перебранка —
но невредимы и горды черты.

The death of God and everything divine
stared from behind those hopeless agate balls.

Without directing its gaze, a star can stare
like that, or what is related to a star
but doesn't have to worry about what makes sense,
being older and off where the open secrets are.

Whatever price we pay for atonement, I doubt
that He will forgive us—He, who dressed the owl
in a shimmering rainbow of browns and dazzling gold
and His own underlay of helpless white.

I snapped out of it. The radio started screaming
greetings to us from every capital.
The comely portraits of faces with wicked features
were smiling right and left all over the place.

Before I left the painter's house, I managed
to say to him, "Good-bye, dear *maître*. May I ask
how come you're here? With your talent, what allowances
you must make for being here at the end of the line!"

Instead of sunset, a rosy mark of some
undefinable color shone a while, then went out,
like the question that waited and waited for an answer
but couldn't wait long enough and finally left us.

Was the star alive, I wondered, that lingered on
in front of me and everywhere around?
Or like the valiant bird did it know how
to be at once both beautiful and dead?

Death: an entry hall, two ugly people's
squabble—but the features intact and proud.

Брезгливости посмертная осанка —
последний труд и подвиг красоты.

В ночи трудился сотворитель чучел.
К нему с усмешкой придвигался ад.
Вопль возносился: то крушил и мучил
сестру кривую синегорбый брат.

То мыслью занимаюсь я, то ленью.
Не время ль съехать в прежний неуют?
Всё медлю я. Всё этот край жалею.
Всё кажется, что здесь меня убьют.

The body showing disgust by its posthumous bearing
is beauty's ultimate labor and heroic deed.

The taxidermist had worked late into the night.
Hell with a sneer had kept creeping closer and closer:
there had risen a terrible wail as the blue-humped brother
bashed and tortured his crooked one-eyed sister.

Some days I think about things; some days, I do nothing.
Perhaps it's time to return to my former bleak life?
Still I dawdle. Still this land makes me feel sorry.
Still I imagine that here I will some day be killed.

Всех обожаний бедствие огромно.
И не совпасть, и связи не прервать.
Так навсегда, что даже у надгробья, —
потупившись, не смея быть при Вас, —
изъявленную внятно, но не грозно
надземную приемлю неприязнь.

При веяньях залива, при закате
стою, как нищий, согнанный с крыльца.
Но это лишь усмешка, не проклятье.
Крест благородней, чем чугун креста.
Ирония — избранников занятье.
Туманна окончательность конца.

[THE FOG]

All means of adoration cause great pain.
Never to coincide nor lose the bond.
Like that forever; so, even at my grave—
my eyes cast down, not bearing to be near You—
I accept the clear, articulate
hostility offered overground.

The wind comes over the gulf; the sun goes down;
I stand like a beggar driven from the porch.
Grinning only—not cursing back.
The cross is nobler than its iron cast.
Irony is the avocation of the elect.
The finality of the end is lost in fog.

Ночь: белый сонм колонн надводных. Никого нет,
но воздуха и вод удвоен гласный звук,
как если б кто-то был и вымолвил: Коонен...
О ком он? Сонм колонн меж белых твердей двух.

Я помню голос тот, не родственный канонам
всех горл: он одинок единогласья средь,
он плоской высоте приходится каньоном,
и зренью приоткрыт многопородный срез.

Я слышала его на поминанье Блока.
(Как грубо молода в ту пору я была.)
Из перьев синих птиц, чья вотчина — эпоха
былая, в дне чужом нахохлилось боа.

Ни перьев синих птиц, ни поминанья Блока
уныньем горловым — понять я не могла.
Но сколько лет прошло! Когда боа поблёкло,
рок маленький ко мне послал его крыла.

Оо, какой простор! Но кто сказал: Коонен?
Акцент долгот присущ волнам и валунам.
Аа — таков ответ незримых колоколен.
То — эхо возвратил недальний Валаам.

[THE ECHO]

Night: white throng of columns on the water. No one here.
Now the public vowel of water and of air reduplicates
as if there were some person near who uttered: Koönen . . .
Who? Whom? Throng of columns between two worlds of white.

I recall that voice, not kindred to the canons
sung by all: in harmony it stands alone.
It is related to a mesa like a canyon,
a many-strain cross section glimpsed but not yet known.

I remember hearing it at services for Blok.
(Back at that time how young and vulgar I was.)
A boa of blue feathers (the bygone age was their
family inheritance) ruffled up that alien day.

I failed to understand the feathers of blue birds
and the mournful singing of the services for Blok.
But how much time has passed! When the boa faded,
its wings came down to me by a vagary of fate.

"Oö," how much free range! Who was it said, "Koönen"?
Long sounds are natural for waves and giant boulders.
"Aä" is what comes back from the bell towers far away.
So here was Balaam, then, echoing what we say.

Я думала, что ты мой враг,
что ты беда моя тяжелая,
а ты не враг, ты просто враль
и вся игра твоя — дешевая.

На площади Манежной
бросал монету в снег.
Загадывал монетой,
люблю я или нет.

И шарфом ноги мне обматывал
там, в Александровском саду,
и руки грел, а все обманывал,
все думал, что и я солгу.

Кружилось надо мной враньё,
похожее на воронье.

Но вот в последний раз прощаешься,
в глазах ни сине, ни черно.
О, проживешь, не опечалишься,
а мне и вовсе ничего.

Но как же все напрасно,
но как же все нелепо!
Тебе идти направо.
Мне идти налево.

I thought you were my enemy,
my terrible calamity,
but no, you're not—you have a line,
and you've been stringing me along.

Remember how in Manège Square
you tossed money in the snow
and tried to get the coins to say
does she love me, yes or no?

Who wrapped whose scarf around my legs
in the Alexander Garden? You!
And warmed my hands and kept pretending,
always thinking that I'd lie, too.

All that lying wove a web
like a flock of crows overhead.

So now you're really saying good-bye,
your eyes not evil, no, nor kind.
Oh, you'll make out—you'll never cry—
and, whatever happens, I don't mind.

What a big mistake it was!
Ridiculous! Inept!
Go; you're going right.
Me, I'm going left.

Всё шхеры, фиорды, ущельных существ
оттуда пригляд, куда вживе не ходят.
Скитания омутно-леший сюжет,
остуда и оторопь, хвоя и холод.

Зажжен и не гаснет светильник сырой.
То — Гамсуна пагуба и поволока.
С налету и смолоду прянешь в силок —
не вырвешь души из его приворота.

Болотный огонь одолел, опалил.
Что — белая ночь? Это имя обманно.
Так назван условно маньяк-аноним,
чьим бредням моя приглянулась бумага.

Он рыщет и свищет, и виснут усы,
и девушке с кухни понятны едва ли
его бормотанья: — Столь грешные сны
страшны или сладостны фрёкен Эдварде?

О фрёкен Эдварда, какая тоска —
над вечно кипящей геенной отвара
помешивать волны, клубить облака —
какая отвага, о фрёкен Эдварда!

И девушка с кухни страшится и ждет.
он сгинул в чащобе — туда и дорога.
Но огненной порчей смущает и жжет
наитье прохладного глаза дурного.

Я знаю! Сама я гоняюсь в лесах
за лаем собаки, за гильзой пустою,

[SORTAVALA]

Nothing but rocky islands, fjords, a concern
for canyons and gorges unenterably bold.
The plot: deep pools and a wood-demon's wanderings,
resentment and madness, conifers and cold.

Now lit, the fog-soaked lampion will not go out.
It gave Hamsun his appeal—and did him harm:
if, young and heedless, you chance upon a snare,
you never work your soul free of its charm.

The swamp fires singed, were overwhelming. Was that
from white nights? False label. That is the name, in truth,
convention gives the anonymous maniac
whose fantasies my blank paper was attracted to.

He roves and rummages and whistles, and
his moustache droops. The kitchen maid finds it hard
to make sense of his mutterings. Are dreams
of sin terrible or sweet, fröken Edvard?

O fröken Edvard, what dreadful pangs of longing—
above the boiling Gehenna of the barley pot
to rile the waters and raise up clouds of steam—
what amazing bravery, O fröken Edvard!

The girl cowers in the kitchen, waits.
He has vanished in the woods beyond the well.
But intuition of a cold and evil eye
troubles the peace with its impassioned spell.

I know about that! I run through woods myself
after a hunting dog, a shell forgotten,

за смехом презренья в отравных устах,
за гибелью сердца, за странной мечтою.

И слышится в сырости мха и хвоща:
— Как скучно! Ничто не однажды, всё — дважды
иль многажды. Ждет не хлыста, а хлыща
звериная душенька фрёкен Эдварды.

Все фрёкен Эдварды во веки веков
бледны от белил захолустной гордыни.
Подале от них и от их муженьков!
Обнимемся, пес, мы свободны отныне.

И — хлыст оставляет рубец на руке.
Пес уши уставил в мой шаг осторожный.
— Смотри, — говорю, — я хожу налегке:
лишь посох, да плащ, да сапог остроносый.

И мне, и тебе, белонощный собрат,
двоюродны люди и ровня — наяды.
Как мы — так никто не глядит на собак.
Мы встретились — и разминемся навряд ли.

Так дивные дива в лесу завелись.
Народ собирался и медлил с облавой —
до разрешенья ответственных лиц
покончить хотя бы с бездомной собакой.

С утра начинает судачить табльдот
о призраках трех, о кострах их наскальных.
И девушка с кухни кофейник прольет
и слепо и тупо взирает на скатерть.

Двоится мой след на росистом крыльце.
Гость-почерк плетет письмена предо мною.

a scornful laugh on poisoned lips, the death
and destruction of my heart, a peculiar dream.

I hear among the musty moss and horsetail,
"So boring! Nothing's only once—it's all
twice again!" Fröken Edvard's wild little soul
anxiously waits not for a whip but a fop.

Bleached by the arrogance of provincial place,
all fröken Edvards are forever pale as sheets.
Stay clear of them, and of their menfolk, too!
Good dog, let's hug; from now on we are free.

The whipping leaves a red welt on my hand.
The dog pricks up its ears at my cautious step.
"Look," I tell it, "I'm traveling light. Just
my crook and cloak and pair of pointed boots."

So you and I, my white-night colleague, are cousins
as people and equals as mountain spirits.
Nobody honors dogs the way we do.
Now that we've met, our paths won't miss each other.

So, in the woods were wonders to behold.
The people gathered round and fanned out slow
until the ones in charge gave their permission
to end the life, at least, of the homeless dog.

At the common breakfast table everyone
starts gossiping about three ghosts, their fires
on the cliff, and the kitchen maid spills the coffee
and stares at the tablecloth with vacant eyes.

My footsteps double on the dewy porch.
My visitor-hand plaits characters before me.

И в новой, чужой, за-озерной красе
лицо провинилось пред явью дневною.

Всё чушь, чешуя, серебристая чудь.
И девушке с кухни до страсти охота
и страшно — крысиного яства чуть-чуть
добавить в унылое зелье компота.

In new, strange beauty now lost beyond the lake
my face offends the reality of day.

Nothing but foolishness, fish scales, Mickey Finns.
And the kitchen maid is filled with a passionate wish—
and yet is afraid—to add just a little rat meat
to the boring potion in the compote dish.

Я завидую ей — молодой
и худой, как рабы на галере:
горячей, чем рабыни в гареме
возжигала зрачок золотой
и глядела, как вместе горели
две зари по-над невской водой.

Это имя, каким называлась,
потому что сама захотела —
нарушенье черты и предела
и востока незваная власть,
так — на северный край чистотела
вдруг — персидской сирени напасть.

Но ее и мое имена
были схожи основой кромешной,
лишь однажды взглянула с усмешкой —
как метелью лицо обмела.
Что же было мне делать — посмевшей
зваться так, как назвали меня?

Я завидую ей — молодой
до печали, но до упаданья
головою в ладонь, до страданья
я завидую ей же — седой
в час, когда не прервали свиданья
две зари по-над невской водой.

Да, как колокол, грузный, седой,
с вещим слухом, окликнутым зовом:
то ли голосом чьим-то, то ль звоном,
излученным звездой и звездой,

I envy the way she was young
and so thin, like the slaves in a galley,
and much hotter than houris in harems
she kindled her golden eye
and looked out at two dawns together
on fire along the Neva.

This name that she went by because
it was the one that she wanted
was a breach of old features and limits
and spoke of the strength of the East,
like a Persian lilac disaster
on a celandine's northern edge.

But her name and mine were alike
on a secret, infernal basis;
only once with a grin she glanced over
like a blizzard sweeping my face.
What could I do, having boldly
accepted the name I was named?

I envy the way she was young
to the point of grieving, but the falling
of the head to the palm and the suffering
I envy her, too, turned gray
the hour two dawns on fire
parted along the Neva.

Like a heavy, gray-haired bell
with prophetic ear and long summons
she speaks with a voice or with ringing
sent out by star after star,

с этим неописуемым зобом,
полным песни, уже неземной.

Я завидую ей — меж корней,
нищей пленнице рая иль ада,
О, когда б я была так богата,
что мне прелесть оставшихся дней?
Но я знаю, какая расплата
за судьбу быть не мною, а ей.

with her indescribable wattle
full of unearthly song.

I envy her deep-rooted ways,
poor captive of hell or of heaven.
If I were that rich would I care for
the delight of remaining days?
Yet I know when a fate like that's reckoned,
it's not I but she who must pay.

ТЕАТР

В. ВЫСОЦКОМУ

Эта смерть не моя есть ущерб и зачёт
жизни кровно-моей, лбом упершейся в стену.
Но когда свои лампы Театр возожжёт
и погасит — Трагедия выйдет на сцену.
Вдруг не поздно сокрыться в заочность кулис?
Не пойду! Спрячу голову в бархатной щели.
Обречённых капризников тщетный каприз —
вжаться,

    вжиться в укромность — вина неужели?
Дайте выжить. Чрезмерен сей скорбный сюжет.
Я не помню из роли ни жеста, ни слова.
Но смеётся суфлёр, вседержитель судеб:
говори: всё я помню, я здесь, я готова.
Говорю: я готова. Я помню. Я здесь.
Сущ и слышим тот голос, что мне подыграет.
Средь безумья, нет, средь слабоумья злодейств
здраво мыслит один: умирающий Гамлет.
Донесётся вослед: не с ума ли сошед
Тот, кто жизнь возлюбил

               да забыл про живучесть.
Дай, Театр, доиграть благородный сюжет,
бледноликий партер повергающий в ужас.

THE THEATER

FOR V. VYSOTSKY

Not mine, this death is both an intimate loss
and a test passed by my life, its head pressed to the wall.
But as soon as the Theater brings up the spots and the
   footlights
and dims the house, the Tragedy comes on.
Is it too late to hide out of sight in the wings?
I won't go! I fold my head in a velvet fall.
This futile whim of doomed, impulsive people
to withdraw,
              to hide in comfort—what's wrong with that?
Better keep living no matter how tragic the theme.
Of my role I can't remember either gesture or line,
but the Almighty prompter laughs at my fate and commands:
"Say, 'I remember it all. I'm here. I'm set.' "
And as I say: "I'm set. I remember. I'm here."
The underlying voice is clear and real.
Caught not in madness but in imbecile evil,
only the dying Hamlet speaks the truth,
and afterward everyone says, "Wasn't he mad
to fall in love with life
              and forget to hang on?"
Come, Theater, act out the noble theme,
plunging the pallid audience in dread.

Prose

A WORD THAT AMOUNTS
TO A DEED

I have been asked, "What kind of a person do you picture your reader?"

Lowering my lids and shading my eyes with my palm, I peer at an appealing, abstract image that I have had my own pupils make up. Under my palm, behind my lids, there glimmers the light of an imaginary lamp, the features of an unknown city begin forming in the window, and someone's kind face slowly comes clear. When this face, self-servingly created by me, who adore beautiful characteristics and expressions, becomes fully real in all its splendor, there's the picture of my ideal reader, and all that remains is to pencil in a volume of Pushkin's, or some other great book, for nothing expressed in the picture has any connection with me. For all my inherent, rhetorical nature, I'm inclined to say straightforwardly that those readers are closest to me who, treating me as simply another reader, agree with me in the main. I'm not one who becomes engrossed in poring over my own lines.

It's absolutely true that inordinate praise, setting me up on a level where I don't belong, even if it flatters my sinful self-esteem, intellectually bores me and alienates me. I'm also stirred and frightened by the excessive fervor of strangers, both men and women, who, aroused by reading poetry, look for an immediate, intimate contact. As a reader, I don't understand that. For some reason, though, it does not at all contradict the fact that, among these agitated readers, I have found some close and even essential participants in my life—something that happened casually, indeed naturally. It is really quite simple: between writer and reader, as between two people in general, there must be neither servility nor excessive familiarity.

If it was necessary for me to fabricate the literarily distanced image of a reader, it was only to enjoy a face bent over a book, focused on what in our consciousness we can subsume under the name Pushkin or what, in other languages and other places, corresponds to it. Like all my colleagues and fellow writers, not only do I have a vital and dependent relationship with my reader even without any obvious signs of his attention or interest, but also I receive many letters and practically every day meet him face to face at my readings or other public appearances, casual or formal. Among the incalculable number of poetry lovers there are those—be they few or be they more—whom I boldly and gratefully call my readers. That simply means that I share with some people a special fondness for our native speech, for the ways in which it intensifies our life and for preserving it unspoiled, and that some people approve the way I work and live in my intention to serve this goal without other motive. There are as many ways as there are poets, and so far mine does not seem to me complete and perfect. But I know that the reader I am talking about supposes, like me, that a word amounts to a deed, and is aware of its moral significance. That fondness for poetry which is expressed as appreciation of me emboldens me and humbles me and keeps my conscience under the proper tension. Regardless of me or my work, especially on distant tours, I have often been struck by the contemporary reader's sophisticated cultural level.

I have met a great number of people who have neither read my books nor heard my name but whose language I was born into, finer and grander than mine, and with whom I am bound my whole life to the last drop of my blood.

I hope to serve life worthily; I have known its blessings; I have been a reader of wonderful books; and I have seen the goodness of people, whom I now, as dawn breaks, with all my heart and mind wish happiness this New Year's Day—and ever after.

January 1, 1976

BABUSHKA

Most often she recurs in my memory as an enormous indefiniteness into which her head and hands gently disappear, as a thick cloud of love gathered above my head but not restricting my freedom. From the time I was little, my grandmother loved me timidly, enthusiastically, never intimately, as if not daring to caress me but, rather, looking on from a distance with huge, yellow-bright eyes, frightening in their passionate expression of goodness and madness, her hands forever half reaching out to me. Only now have they relaxed in their embarrassed, unappeased longing to touch me.

When I was a child, I generally disliked being touched. An angry, impulsive shame would make my skin burn when grownups hugged me or saw me undressed. I was especially deeply ashamed in front of my own family. Toward the few people of my own blood who raised me, I always felt an awkward, morbid clumsiness lacerating, torturing my whole body. Even Roma, my dog, who became so much part of me during my long, lonely, passionate closeness with him, whom I knew so well and who copied everything I did, who could look at me with my grandmother's look of forgiveness, belongs, in some degree, to this oppressive complex taking vengeance on my physical singleness.

For people I did not know I did not have such keen feelings, such bodily sensitivity. Once, a wicked, suspicious man, who had gotten into the house when no one was home except Katya the housekeeper, tried to pat my head with his dirty hand. I disgustedly, haughtily pushed him away. But I felt no shame even when Katya came in and flirtatiously pressed her belly on the windowsill and spread her shapeless legs wrapped in their dark blue pants.

On the other hand, when my mother wanted our picture taken swimming at the shore, me eight years old and naked in her arms, I immediately began running away, stumbling over the stones of the beach at Gudauta, and for a long time gave her an oriental, sullen look, which I was very good at as a child.

But my grandmother, perhaps because of the madness that meekly dwelt in her, with her blind fondness for me, tactfully saw how twisted my fancies were and never provoked my proud and captious chastity. For her it seemed to be enough to embrace the air I walked through, which, for her alone, continued to hold the shape of my body.

The degree of my physical trust for my family was in inverse proportion to my closeness to them: first Babushka, then my Aunt Christina, and then Mama.

I went to the bathhouse only with Babushka, but even then I did not experience the easy freedom of a child getting washed, casually holding out its arms and legs to the washcloth. With the biased eye of a wicked supervisor always seeking the hoped-for flaw and with the soap stinging my eyes, I would glance sideways at Babushka, at her tiny, pitiful body with its enormous, twitching head, her white hair spotted with an unwashable mixture of colors—she was always getting Christina's oil paints on her—and at her unsteady, thin white legs. And having maliciously noticed her unhappily sagging belly and her thin, goat-gray hair, in a sort of angry despair I would butt it with the dun end of the washtub.

Judging by two old snapshots, miraculously preserved, Babushka was very tall, much taller than the well-dressed man with an elegant moustache photographed beside her, impressively and morosely slender, with a powerfully free black swirl of Italian hair and with unfathomable eyes, whose panicky roundness has been focused on an evil premonition of some vain and destructive deed. Her stately, swarthy face expresses obvious concealment of some secret. The way her body leans forward gives a feeling of untrammeled inconvenience, as if she were standing on a high, narrow cornice.

She had four husbands, three children—Elena died in childhood—and one granddaughter. Perhaps because of that ever more simplified one-and-onlyness coming down to me, Babushka, who laid a chill over her husbands and unevenly divided her love between her daughters, with anguish and with a squeal of the brakes applied suddenly on her headlong, easily distracted, loving soul, came to a stop on me. Her intelligence, well organized for a woman of impassioned foolishness (with which she was seriously ill at one point), rebellious, bustling, its imaginative flight not halted by any medical barrier, indefinitely longing for hurdles to overcome, finally calmed down at the lifesaving shock of my coming into the world. Babushka's nerves, which led in so many directions, easily upset by compassion, curiosity, irascibility at things happening, like her affection for everything, finally focused on me, and that through no merit of mine. Even ahead of time, behind my back, unrestrainedly, intensely, and reverentially Babushka fell in love with me on April 10, 1937.

As a child I knew that Babushka had been born long ago in Kazan province. Her grandfather, an Italian organ-grinder, had brought the family name to Russia. Nowadays I wonder what drew him precisely here to suffer; to freeze; to wear out a monkey; with his wild, sullen, southern look to seduce an uncomely young lady and by chance produce a son, Mitrofan— all near Kazan where his strange, yellow, slant-eyed, impossible brother under the same barren sky was already doing what he could, working and laughing, summoning forth his son, Akhmadulla, my paternal great-grandfather. What a long, mutual tunneling the two of them did through pitch-dark fate to come colliding together in me! How many sacrifices there were!

Babushka's father was a doctor, who tended the wounded during the Crimean campaign. Her mother, by the bold and patient efforts of a practical and self-serving cast of mind, acquired noble status and a considerable fortune. As far as I remember what I heard as a child, they had six children—three of each sex. The older sons, willful and daring, made holes with slingshots in the portraits of their not so venerable ancestors, tied Babushka to a table, and went to military school. What happened to those poor, awful, favorite souls I have no idea. The youngest, somewhat phlegmatic and very honest and decent, became a famous revolutionary. Until his death, Babushka kept up only with him, praising him highly, and it struck me that she had an eternally soft spot in her heart for him because he had not tied her leg up. Other people, too, have told me that he was always honest and decent, but I myself never picked up his punctual brilliance.

Babushka's older sisters, Natalya and Mariya Mitrofanovna, were beautiful women who sang superbly, who were very Italian both physically and morally, who for a long time remained locked in maidenhood by their mother's cupidity, and who married tragically. They lived in bursts of bad luck and died after their parents with serious psychological illnesses. My mother remembers one of them when she still was beautiful but already afflicted with illness, her delicate hands greedily twitching to collect, beg, even steal various worthless gewgaws. Apparently, profoundly hurt in her beauty and disinterestedness by the shadow of those great luminaries Life, Love, and Hope that had fallen on her, she trusted only the world's small, harmless suns—tin cans, glass baubles, candy silver, mirror fragments—comforted by their humble, childish sheen. Although any sickness in her had long gone, Babushka also preserved a passion for trifles, but she strictly chose only those that seemed to her distinguished by some trace of me: my little boxes, my candy wrappers, scraps of my drawings, my notes of thanks printed in capital letters to the many animals of my childhood. Even now all this is in some one place, or else it vanished with her who so miserly and so fondly saved it.

Babushka was the ugly, unloved, and youngest child in the family. Probably her mother had by her time become tired of struggling, of putting up with the burdens of running a house, of admitting sharp, wounding Italian blood into her body and cutting it with her thin, lower-middle-class Russian blood to mitigate the effects of dark eyes and madness in future children, all of whom disappointed and alienated her by their failures. I think that by her authoritatively and evenhandedly taking part in her descendants' lives, she managed partly to rescue and partly to alter their fates. Thanks to her sober healthiness, madness in our family was always inconclusive, kept in equilibrium by the prevailing scarcities of daily life, the pupils' terrifying blackness touched up by an easygoing sallowness of complexion, the eyes' incredible, disastrous demands met head-on by futility and boredom. But I still hope—perhaps!—that my father's fresh Asianness, forcefully introduced into this muddle of bloods, will liberate me from her sometimes rash, sometimes cautious semiwitchery and let me live and die far beyond the borders of the tameness she plucked from tragedy!

When she was a young high-school student, with all the ardor of a lonely child's introvertedness, Babushka took a liking to an older girl, who extended condescending protection, called her "my protégette," and then in everybody's hearing made fun of Babushka's childhood diaries entrusted in a burst of gratitude. Such things happen to all children, but Babushka never outgrew her quiet, almost holy foollike inoffensiveness that invariably provoked vicious displays by older, stronger figures. By the end of her life, the more fantastic and ludicrous her goodness and her meekness became, the more furiously neighbors and passersby were enraged and amused, teasing her for her distractingly elevated speech, fastidiously avoiding her collection of animals, even scorning her indifference toward food, which Babushka tried to overcome in the kitchen but always came out conquered by the unequal encounter with pots and pans.

At some point in her youth, Babushka had been governess for the Zalesskys, rich, cheerful people who kept forgetting to put her down. Only their youngest daughter, Zinaida, somewhat bothered Babushka by a sharp temper and the surprises of an early and cheekily mature physical nature. Babushka once recalled this, but for some reason I, too, remember their name, the carefree house and huge garden leading down to the river, and how once they set out on a picnic in rowboats without Babushka and Zinaida, and Zinaida, standing in the wind on the hilltop, shouted after them, "I, Zinaida Zalesskaya, fifteen years old, wish to go in the boat!" And when, without heeding her, they disappeared from sight, she yelled with gay arrogance, yanking at the hooks closing the cambric of her shirt, "Idiots! Look! I have breasts and everything else grown-up and lots better than Mademoiselle Nadine!"

Babushka distinctly remembered and admired everything that contradicted her humble silence, apparently longing for the impetuousness handed down to her from the wild south by the organ-grinder and forbidden by her mother's severe temperance. For my part, I have not forgotten this little episode because he lived where I wanted to—in the very house, in the very garden, in the only land that has struck me with profound nostalgia and is unrecognizable through my beloved literature yet is one I seem to recall, like some ancient pre-life in the cradle from which I was stolen by nomads.

Under her good brother's influence, supporting her in her solitary depression, Babushka broke sharply with the family and went off to Kazan to study to be a medical assistant. (I cite the details of her life as best I recall them not because the events seem to me effective or remarkable but rather out of respect for that aureole of significant pitifulness palely hovering over us all, over the scanty semidarkness of our life's dramas, and also because I would like to make clear how Babushka's image, shorn of any bright, cutting edge, acutely and deeply stunned my sight and often gently stopped me from being conceited or doing something nasty.) She got carried away by ideas of freedom and equality, took part in meetings and May Day outings, hid proclamations in her corset, and chaired a short-lived revolutionary circle.

Two female comrades from that circle more than a half century later looked Babushka up and called on her in her long, narrow, cold room meant to harden a person to the discomforts of the cemetery. Prim, in formal black, the sempiternal old ladies in squeamish fright stepped over the sill into Babushka's disorder, raising their hems above the dangerous swamp of the floor populated by the vermin among our wild animals. Angered by the depth of her fall, as if it had cast a shadow over them, they spoke to Babushka sternly and didactically, belligerently persuaded her to obtain a pension increase, their black boots shining all the while like varnished revolvers. She fearlessly flew around them on devilish fustian wings, babbling emotionally and not listening, assenting to everything with an uncertain jerk of her head, set pale tea before them, candies all stuck together like a honeycomb, liverwurst meant for the cat, and a moment later took it all away, freeing their hands for my child's drawings and poems. And to top it off, first announced—preparing them for a delightful shock—then brought in little, sullen me as the craftily concealed (until the right moment) but all-clarifying proof of her blinding and extraordinary well-being. They coolly and calmly fixed their eyes on my frowning, butting forehead and simultaneously shot the sharp arrows of their palms at me. This obviously somewhat lowered them in Babushka's opinion, because she suddenly looked at them through the darkened yellowness of her pupils with the clear and cheerful erudition of lofty superiority. We saw them out to the stairs, and Babushka was happily babbling again and decrepitly leaning over after them, her breath making little clouds above two stiff, black figures folded up like umbrellas.

Young Babushka was frequently imprisoned: for slips of the tongue or for slander, for an inability to protect herself from the unexpectednesses of being shadowed and searched, for a tendency to take on herself, with joyfully and distractedly big eyes, the whole responsibility for revolutionary acts. The police persistently and patiently, like taking matches from children, constantly took away Babushka's false-bottomed suitcases and, with a habitual gesture—*Pardon, Mademoiselle!*—extracted from

157

the warm confines of her collar cigarette paper addressed to the workers of the world.

Ugly, unloved, and last Babushka was born; so she grew up and, in her unprepossessing, timid way of carrying herself, lived her long life. A childish fear of her own undesirability and onerousness even in her old age gave her face a diffident, guilty, bashful expression.

Above all, in a terrible way, before her head and hands began shaking, Babushka fussily feared drawing to herself the least bit of attention or, in her slightly hunchbacked thinness, taking up space others needed to move around in. As she got older, she became smaller and smaller, as if deliberately turning into a legendary and ideal bagatelle that no one needed and that got in no one's way, something she has now achieved as a meager handful of dust in the tiny, iconless shelter of her last resting place.

Despite my mother's making scenes, Babushka insistently and secretly hardly ate anything, as if ashamed to do out of its fair share the eternally open, demanding, insatiable mouth of some unknown nestling. To buy off the greediness of some strange hunger oppressing her, she would feed emaciated, wiry alley cats flying with a screech over the dismal rubbish heap in the courtyard and a gluttonous bird horde on the windowsill.

To my mother's displeasure and embarrassment in front of neighbors, Babushka wore an unchangeable, gnomic, unkempt, coarse-cloth, shirt dress, in winter weather reinforced by additional old rags, and slept on a devoutly and aggressively preserved piece of gray cloth worn thin by washing—for eighty years atoning for the sin of worn-out diapers and baby shirts sullenly counted by her mother, who intensely feared the demise of property that she herself had brought forth in labor.

That stern, inflexible mother let drunks and madmen have ever greater run of the dying estate, and their chorus line cruelly closed around her acts of clear thinking, and she went down, confounding her unmerciful, domineering legs, in order to hold the huge head of her unloved child to her breast.

Babushka fictitiously married a young revolutionary, a step necessary for him to obtain permission to leave the country, and she forever kept the name given her by this sad wedding of convenience. She took him abroad, but Switzerland only worsened the illness that was picking on the lungs of passionate young people. They had to return posthaste, but at this point in her story comes something vague and suspicious about the necessary money having been squandered by some comrades who then through decades of good fortune outlived the victim of their carelessness; Babushka never mentioned it. She and her husband ended up in the south of Russia as politically unreliable people; when the tsar was traveling through they were jailed for three days, where, unrestrainedly, her first husband's blood gave out.

All this was at the beginning of the century, before the 1905 revolution, and it marks the beginning, at least according to my childhood view of things, of Babushka's unexciting, drowsy downhill slide. Probably I did not properly appreciate her sad keenness and self-reliance; in Nizhny Novgorod she gave birth to Christina, was completely rejected by her family, and, penniless, set out for the Donbass to help in a cholera epidemic. She was there a long time, working and living in a wing of a hospital, subjecting her older daughter to constant danger, and, a few years later, having Mama (Mama in turn got all the illnesses of the people Babushka was taking care of). Babushka's fourth husband—the one with the moustache—loved her deeply, giving up his middle-class status, adopting her daughters, and being a good father to them until he, too, became lost in the fog swallowing up all lines of Babushka's fate. Babushka raised her daughters as well as she could, taught them drawing, foreign languages, and music, all of which neither of them inclined to. Christina mastered nothing, not even painting, which she dumbly loved all her life, but Mama, by the great efforts of her little, illness-wracked body, everything. Only Christina knew how to love, pity, and forgive. Naturally, life in such a dull, impoverished mine could not get along without an incurably ungovernable woman from time to time bursting into the repulsive hospital courtyard: nude, in a huge, demonic whirlwind of hair, she would appear in the dusty sunlight of a moment's freedom so that her wild cry of "Get thee behind me, Satan!" would resound through my mother and my aunt's childhood and, by reproduction of that terrible *i*-sound forewarning of an excruciating and unbearable yoke, even scare me: "Behi-i-i-nd!"

The fact that Babushka was a "nurse"—"for whom?" "for anyone who needs her"—was something that in early childhood I understood and took advantage of. To her nursing kindness I dragged a whole slew of feeble, ugly creatures that my mother had turned away: a white puppy with an enormous pink belly, a blind guinea pig, a rabbit with broken legs, cats, wingless birds, and other crippled animals whose tiny bodies seemed hugely superfluous among the world's surplus and humbly existed outside their species. Babushka admitted them all to her dark nest, showing them all the equal homage they had earned by having been born. From her, now dead, I learned to say with tender respect in a singsong voice of wonder, "Alive!"—and therefore something fragile, defenseless, needing help and compassion. One time, when the beating of little pulses inhabiting her room threatened to grow into a mighty roar, I bought and brought home a baby chick that had just been incubated, and Mama, by refusing to let me go to Babushka's, seemed to slam the door in my face forever with that invincible strictness that from time to time overcame her and about which there was nothing to be done. Drooping my tear-stained head, I slowly went downstairs and sat down on the floor behind the door, with my palm sheltering the teeny yellowness condemned and cursed by the big world. I heard my father walking overhead, other mothers calling other children, and I began fearfully to imagine that I would sit there forever, imprisoned between the wall and the door. Forty years later I remember how I had the complex but passionate idea of throttling the little, breathing throat, and how I set my two fingers in a ring around the narrow rivulet of blood and air defenselessly coursing through it. But my fingers would not close. Once and for all, I joyfully began to weep anew over my own and everybody else's salvation, and in thanks to God at that instant Babushka, who had been looking for me, was leaning over me. She immediately carried me and the baby chick off to the redemptive heaven of her love, filled with the smell of old rags and little animals.

Returning from wartime evacuation, we all were very much afraid of rats, even after we had long solicited them to let us live in our own houses, and at night we felt the piercing twin fires of their eyes presaging no good, but Babushka and I managed to forgive them, too. A soldier guarding a nearby building, ridiculing our childish fright, kicked a huge, chestnut-colored, bloody, half-dead rat out with his boot. Left alone with it on the narrow street, looking up distrustfully at the jeering soldier, I triumphed over my body's shuddering, bent down close, and picked it up. The rat looked at me brightly with a monumental hatred worthy of a beautiful, strong animal, as if precisely this loathing of me was the cause of its death. I took it along with me in the only direction in which my freedom was unlimited, and, most likely, my pure pity for a living thing was strengthened by my gloating self-mockery and, toward Babushka, a kind of malicious desire to make fun of and to test out her universal goodness. Having no such complex motives herself, Babushka was neither angry nor surprised when she saw me with the dying rat in my hands and took us in with a clear, single-minded sigh of compassion.

Even now Babushka's poor little ark is afloat and reaches shore though abandoned by her and no longer steered by scatter-brained little old Christina, who saved a pale pink cat named Petya and a whole tribe of medium-sized babbling pigeons.

It was not so much that Babushka was generous as that her

whole organism, light, simple, and limited by the ailment of eccentricity, included in the last quarters of its waning moon only what really mattered—love and good deeds—without adding such secondary instincts as caution, thrift, envy, and spite.

She was superstitiously oppressed by every comfort or convenience, even putting her miserable pension into a thick book for Christina and me on children's diseases, a book kept in plain sight. How well I remember its readily opening to a page showing a sick, withered child with a drooping head and an obvious abundance of ribs and bones that could not help it stand. There, too, all Babushka's wealth was kept as if offered as sacrifice to that little ill god deserving of the world's pity. For ages, Babushka had had no key, and once somebody mockingly robbed that sickly, secret child.

At one point one summer, using my holiday spending money, I acquired a dozen silver Christmas tree elephants—a large quantity of identical objects that for some reason maddeningly, irresistibly tickled me pink. Criticized and laughed at by everyone, with a lonely howl I buried my head in Babushka's lap, and she, first playing up to my childish craziness and then to the craziness of her older sisters, ecstatically stared at the stupid, wild elephantine silver, inconsistently praising my find. We bought eight more, impoverishing the rickety god—whistling and sparkling began in my head—and, choking with laughter, we started getting rid of them or quietly passing them out to children in Ilinsky Square, but almost no one wanted them, and Babushka, alarmed, scooted off with me, shuffling her old scruffy shoes.

Probably it is not my virtue that drives me, drunk or sober, to free myself of the easy burden of property but Babushka's cheerful unwillingness to tie herself down with possessions.

Until the penultimate moment, Babushka read much and well, simply and accurately discriminating among good and bad books with her weak eyes much magnified by her lenses and often changed in color, now made light blue by cataracts. She judged what she read or heard not intellectually but by the limitation on good, which makes it illiterate about evil. By and large she knew and used only vivid words that stood for something, whose trustworthiness was obvious to the touch. All vain, abstract speech flowed around her like another language. When a committee came from Mama's job to check on and evaluate my upbringing, Babushka respectfully, intently, and at length lent her ear to a diction difficult for her, as being not-music, and suddenly, with her whole body grasping the real meaning of my name, understood everything in a flash and, terrifyingly shaking her head, resuming the sickness in her voice, shouted, "Get out!"

Babushka was constantly enraptured by me but was less surprised by my rare successes than others were, seeming to have foreseen them and exaggerated them ahead of time. Whatever happens to me I will never seem to anyone so beautiful and so much to be looked at, unless his vision be dulled by love's swoon and his lids be wet and darkened.

The last time I saw Babushka was after a long interval and when she was already mortally ill, her body halfway between life and death, all her old habits overcome: clean, in clean linen, with a small, clean, tranquil head, Babushka lay eating puréed fruit with a little spoon, fruit she used to think healthful and edible only by me.

"Wait a minute," Christina whispered, coming in front of me. "I'll first warn her." But for some while she could not make up her mind to do so, afraid that my name, which had always excited Babushka, would now be bad for her. "Mama," Christina said cautiously and tenderly, "don't get excited, but Bellochka has come. . . ."

"Ah," responded Babushka indifferently with half her lips and voice.

And suddenly I realized my worst, unbearable fear, that Christina would go away, and I would see, and there would be not my old Babushka, who would not let me see this Babushka as she never allowed anything painful or frightening.

Nevertheless, I sat down on the edge of her clean bed and blindly kissed her new, clean scent.

"I'll soon die," Babushka said captiously and almost coquettishly, but for me nothing made any difference in this first, full depth of loss turning my consciousness to stone.

For an instant, Babushka's good side, where her heart was beating its powerful utmost as it was dying, shuddered feebly, intentionally reached out to me in incomplete affection, and one huge, immortally loving eye turned back to me from the depths of far away.

"Go, I'm tired," Babushka said as if bored, and added, "Take it away," referring to a fond but tarnished Petya huddling up against her.

Evidently, everything that she had loved and felt sorry for so long had now become wearying for her, or, on the contrary, she had still not grown weary of loving and feeling sorry for us and was therefore now pushing us away from herself.

AN ETERNAL PRESENCE

At first there was only the sound "Boo-boo-boo." This was Babushka's big lips burbling on top of a little child's unsteady head, informing it of truth to come and of the joy granted everyone for no reason at all but merely in recognition of having been born. Later, during the orphanhood of the wartime evacuation, the mumbling clarified into words, whose affectionate and inescapable awe frighten me to this day: "Gale winds cover the sky in gloom . . ."

Many years later in Trigorskoe, in gale and gloom, by the light of a three-candle candlestick, as if by itself unwinding the mechanism of the last century, a little gold bird, the joy and delight of solitary winter evenings, bursts into tears in its cage. Perhaps it was not here then; so much the worse! How he pined, how poor he was in these snow-covered places.

Between these two experiences a lot happened—I went from a first, carefree possession by Pushkin to separation from him during my adolescent, rebellious ignorance. As we grow older and wiser, our spirit turns again to Pushkin, passionately takes after him, draws him to itself, a quest which corresponds to our own quest for maturity. What a pleasure to appropriate this figure without expropriating anyone else, to establish personal contact with the most captivating individual of mankind, as cheerfully healthy and unblemished as a winter day. By the way, a description of such a winter day with its frost and sunlight and charming, unnamed friend is for us all sufficient ground not to plumb the land of grief.

To admire him is difficult; the mystery of his entirely unrestrained gracefulness is excruciating. Where does such freedom focused in the throat come from?

Drawing near Izhory station,
I beheld the vaulted skies . . .

Or rather, this gracefulness and this freedom were famous, and for it what did he get but driven into a corner, his common sense burned, and a bullet wound in his lower abdomen? And so we wander back and forth between the joy that he is alive and wondrously beautiful and the terrible news of his death, always fresh and casting a pall over our vision.

> *And remembered your expressions,*
> *Your enchanting dark blue eyes.*

How is it done? Sometimes it seems that only A. N. Vulf understood, he who considered himself an accomplice to the poem*—oh, let him; that is probably how it was. But who was Pushkin with? Traveling along with good-for-nothing Aleksei Nikolaevich, credulously beaming brightly, drawing near Izhory station, and not a trace of me anywhere. O horror of longing and jealousy.

There was a lot of jealousy of Pushkin, as there always is. We are all in love and jealous, like the nice, extended Osipov-Vulf family—jealous of friends, lovers, researchers, professional readers, of all who infringe on Pushkin's belonging only to our heart and mind.

We all expect something, hope to get something from Pushkin—after all, he never refuses to reply. It is enough to focus on him one's spirit unencumbered by evil in order to perceive the salutary sound of his appearance, no more noticeable than the beginning of a smile or a blush. But one should not be too familiar with his name. He knows what we owe him and, at one go, will put us in place with the exultant unceremoniousness permitted only to him—he need ask nobody's permission:

---

*Pushkin met the poem's addressee, E. V. Belyasheva, Aleksei Vulf's cousin, on Vulf's estate "Raspberry-canes" at Izhory neary Petersburg.

The reader wants the rhyme-word roses . . .†

So we stand there with our stupid expression having caught his gallant and offhand rose in midair—as a present or as a gibe.

We are travelers in Pushkin's direction, and although we follow a path of our own intellect and our own morality, geographically we are led to his Mikhailovskoe; where should Pushkin be if not here? The curator of national preserves, or director of the national park, S. S. Geichenko, says that you must know how to summon the one who saturated the air of park, forest, and field with his visible presence, and then he will immediately reply, "Halloo!" Dear Semyon Stepanovich, judging by your poly-mathic face that has had a look into the mystery, you have often had the good luck to get that call back.

So then, suffering, a wound and death affirmed by the im-mutability of a white monument behind a monastery fence are not enough for Pushkin to be absent from the world?

But now we are talking only about the fact that Pushkin was born, and to celebrate it we have a national holiday—but what more should the people who gave birth to this child do on this day?

I imagine that white storks living above the country-house entrance are anxiously casting a sharp eye on the huge crowd.

A large number of people unified by well-informed affection are properly referred to as mankind. To which of its lucky ones is the "Halloo!" directed, sprinkled vaguely throughout the park as if in reciprocal friendliness—Pushkin's greeting to us?

He died, a century passed, plus as many years as I was old

---

†The line is from *Evgeny Onegin*, chapter 4, stanza 42:

> *The ringing frost is freezing noses*
> *And shining silver in the fields;*
> *(The reader wants the rhyme-word* roses;
> *There; take it, will you please!)*

when, one evening last August after a rainstorm, I gloomily stopped in the middle of the park where once upon a time he used to walk every day. Where the path turned I had just run into a quick, stiff wind, which had no reason to be there in that lovely weather. Probably the air stirred up a century and a half ago by his frenzied childish running was still whirling and whistling through the whole place. Annoyed, as if he, in fact running past me, had bumped me with his elbow, I turned and went back.

What with the speed of his movements, he laid his spirit and shadow over everything here, and it has been impossible not to find remembrances of him: my foot kept falling into his tracks. Nevertheless, the feeling of coinciding with him was artificial and inaccurate.

In order completely to re-create in my mind a moment of his vision, I calculatingly headed for the spot where it was most plausible—to the spring he loved to look at. An impatient desire to get something from it overcame me. I was tired of thinking about him, of tracing his breath as it still hung in space; my excitement craved tangible results and reciprocity.

I came from the side where the bushes are in order to catch the bare marble figure from behind and unawares, knowing it had to be the mediator between his mood and mine. I passionately expected it to look back at me with the energy of his eyes assumed by the dark-faced stone at the beginning of the last century. Taking ardent mental delusion as the cutting edge of perfect gain, I mightily aimed it at the statue's features and right away understood that I had missed, like a person kissing empty air.

Of course, he stood precisely here, in August, one evening, after a rainstorm, and he saw the youthful unconsciousness of this body, the plain face with the faint expression of some half-surmise, the delicate, lowered shoulder, the pointed breast, the unsophisticated knees open to the maple leaves' moist falling. Enough of him! The whole thing did not matter to me at all.

168

At once weary and bored, I walked around one more time just in case, sometimes tilting my head, sometimes sullenly peering from under my brow, but still I experienced absolutely no response. I cupped some cold water in my palm and drank; it was flat and tasteless; and suddenly feeling malice and anger, I briskly set out to leave.

But gradually my nerves refocused on him, and the influence of his park tormentingly directed me, like powerful eyes on my back, making my movements seem restricted and intoxicated. I blindly, cunningly made my way forward through the orange glory of the setting sun, out of my mind from a powerful premonition, all attention and on point, like a hunting dog that has closed off sound and sight so its nostrils may better catch the intimate ache of the sought-for scent. Then, through the keen foresight of the shoulder blades, I caught the subtle signal of a greeting solicitously directed to me. Slowing down, in the triumphant silence of my pulse, I turned round to these trees, to this sky and the water, to the statues intelligently showing white among the green, to everything that suddenly had not withheld the fullness of his name and in longing and in love had breathed it to the back of my head.

A small building with a chorus line of columns beside a rounded entrance shimmered distinctly in the deep twilit distance. Responding to the summons of the bright whiteness, I went up to it and in the sand next to the steps made out the sharp print of a small foot, sly and quick like a smile. Laughing gaily, I rubbed my brow, like a cat, on the kind coolness of the columns, attaining simplicity and peace. I knew who had set them up so impartially and truly, and I thanked him for his lucidity of mind. The unworried freedom of the elongated building was checked by the stern, firm discipline of the columns, and my spirit rested in their measured order as under the protection of a simple law. Probably, the one on whose behalf I had come used to rest there from his burning but vague, hot-tempered young brain, leaning his strong forehead

169

against the sober maturity of the marble semicircles. His image that so wore me out that day grew quiet and let go its insistence, and I could take my leave of it with the pleasant sense of having won.

I returned to town and slept wonderfully in a small, old-fashioned hotel room, even in my dreams delighting in its peaceful ivy and useless brass candelabra.

In the morning I visited the house where he lived and died and, tying big slippers on over my shoes, went up to the small apartment many times restored but nevertheless well preserving a sense of trouble. Several visitors, their hands shyly behind their backs and keeping a distance, stretched their heads out toward the many stands, and in this cautious pose they all seemed long-nosed and touchingly unattractive.

I immediately fell into a sense of being apart from him, as if, contrary to my expectations, I had not found him home. All his pictures and copies of his letters and documents did not reveal the point or purport of his mystery but, on the contrary, carried me farther away toward the alien and generally accepted explanation of his personality as a great man.

In one room I ran into a large group of tourists headed by one of the museum's docents. In a confident voice she was listing the sad things of his life, faultlessly putting her pointer on debts, jealousy, loneliness, the ever more exacerbated dead end of his last days. I could not stand listening to it; briefly glancing at me, she apparently noticed disobedience to truth in my expression and an independence of affection not subject to her imperious will. With malicious obstinacy she began directing her explanations to me, and I, caught in awkward dependency on her fierce look, could not leave. Appreciating my meekness and somewhat relaxing, she, as if to sing, raised her voice to inform me of his tragic death, but I, with the unexpected ease of an animal, turned my back on her and went out.

At that point I hurried on to avoid the group, but the scholarly lady was not satisfied to punish me with a look; I heard breathing and tramping behind me as she urged the chase on.

Nevertheless, I paused beside a modest case containing under glass half a meter of soft, black material cut by a tailor to an elegant, exact silhouette. This was the vest the great man had put on the morning of the fatal day. His gracefully small size surprised and moved me, and the living strength of my body shuddered in powerful compassion, ready to leap forward to shield his kindred, fervent, defenseless thinness. But it was too late long ago, and tears of pity and bewilderment got in the way of my looking.

Downstairs in the courtyard, where outbuildings and lilac still existed in the humble comfort of bygone centuries, a strange little girl joyfully fixed her attention on me and said with heartfelt affection, "Hi, there." I thought this a good sign and hurried to get going, as if he were waiting for me and I knew where.

Then when I realized I would soon be driving away, I walked slowly in order to exhaust myself with the town and not regret parting. It was too simply put together not to notice this. Each of its streets, shining with logic and directness, demanded an artistic solution and oppressed reason with the ceaseless labor of rapture. The very old buildings, filled with contemporary daily life, seemed to me unreal and uninhabitable, like the Parthenon, and leaning my head toward their bright façades, I experienced the dark anxiety of an ignoramus spiraling into the heavens. He whose footprints had led me to this place loved this town lightly and easily: for him, perfection was the humdrum and involuntary version of form; no other conception ever entered his head.